A DOUBLE LIFE
AND THE
DETECTIVES.

A

DOUBLE LIFE

AND

THE DETECTIVES.

BY
ALLAN PINKERTON

Black Squirrel Books® 🐿®

an imprint of The Kent State University Press

Kent, Ohio 44242   www.KentStateUniversityPress.com

BLACK SQUIRREL BOOKS® 🐿®

Frisky, industrious black squirrels are a familiar sight on the Kent State University campus and the inspiration for Black Squirrel Books®, a trade imprint of **The Kent State University Press.**

www.KentStateUniversityPress.com

Published by The Kent State University Press, Kent, Ohio 44242
All rights reserved
ISBN 978-1-60635-433-9
Manufactured in the United States of America

First published by G. W. Carleton & Co., Publishers, New York, 1884.

Cataloging information for this title is available at the Library of Congress.

25 24 23 22 21   5 4 3 2 1

PUBLISHER'S NOTE
The Kent State University Press

———

In bringing you these Pinkerton Detective Stories in new facsimile editions, we hope to accomplish several purposes:

- To highlight the breadth and depth of the Borowitz Collection within the Kent State University Special Collections and Archives. These original Pinkerton editions are part of a vast collection of true crime and detective materials, including books, pamphlets, broadsides, and other artifacts. Please visit https://www.library.kent.edu/special-collections and-archives /borowitz-collection to browse this amazing resource.
- To choose good stories, highlighting the longstanding popularity of the detective genre, particularly in American culture. Both nonfiction and fiction books have a strong hold on our cultural imagination, and these Pinkerton books—like many, but perhaps even more than most—are classified as nonfiction but obviously have a strong fictional component. With the Pinkerton National Detective Agency existing as an ongoing entity, the promotional element of these books cannot really be overstated.

- To add to our understanding of the late nineteenth century, a time of great historical importance in American history. While we must remember that the Pinkerton books have a fictional component, they also represent significant episodes, movements, and attitudes of the late 1800s.

In thinking about this last purpose, in particular, it's important to provide a bit of context. One should keep in mind that the books include racial, ethnic, and gender stereotypes too widely prevalent during this period in history; indeed, some of the language and depictions of individuals are not only unfair but offensive. As all too representative of that time, it's remarkable to see how matter of factly such characterizations are presented. In addition, one must understand that the Pinkerton Agency—in these books presented as the absolute "good guys"—are known to have used underhanded tactics, violence, and even illegal methods as a matter of course. Just a few years prior to the publication of *The Railroad Forger and the Detectives,* for instance, Pinkerton agents worked as infiltrators in the open conflict of the Great Railroad strike of 1877, which left over 100 people dead.

Much has been written about the Pinkertons recently, including fine articles in *Grunge* and *Teen Vogue.* The Agency and its motto, "We Never Sleep," are a part of our cultural consciousness; thus, a look at these books, with all the context and backstory pulled close, is both interesting and instructive.

Happy reading.

EXPLORING THE BOROWITZ COLLECTION

Cara Gilgenbach
Special Collections and Archives, Kent State University

The Borowitz Collection, from which the editions of the Pinkerton detective stories are taken, was officially gifted to Kent State University in 1989 by Albert and Helen Borowitz of Cleveland, Ohio. The collection includes primary and secondary sources on crime as well as works of literature based on true crime incidents.

Albert and Helen Borowitz, both scholars themselves, built a scholarly collection—one that affords more than sufficient breadth and depth to support any number of research inquiries. The Borowitz Collection reflects the multidisciplinary expertise of Albert Borowitz (a Harvard graduate with degrees in classics, Chinese regional studies, and law) and his late wife, Helen Osterman Borowitz (a Radcliffe graduate and art historian with literary interests). In addition to collecting, Albert Borowitz is himself a scholar of true crime, having published over a dozen books and many articles on the topic, most notably his masterwork, *Blood and Ink: An International Guide to Fact-Based Crime Literature.*

The Borowitz collection is an extensive one, documenting the history of crime, with primary emphasis on the United States, England, France, and Germany from ancient times to the present day. It includes groups of materials on specific criminal cases that have had notable impacts on art, literature, and social attitudes. This provides the researcher with a wealth of material on those cases and their cultural effects. The collection includes nearly 15,000 volumes of books and periodicals, complemented by archival and manuscript collections. Special areas of note include an excellent collection of Sherlock Holmes and other Arthur Conan Doyle early editions; nonfiction and fiction works related to Jack the Ripper; nineteenth- and twentieth-century British and American crime pamphlets and broadsides; a Wild West collection; crime-related photographs, playbills, postcards, and other ephemera; and artifacts, graphics, and memorabilia related to crime.

The Borowitz Collection includes numerous works of detective stories, both fiction and nonfiction, including books from the Pinkerton Detective Agency series, which embody the collection's central theme, namely how real-life elements of crime infiltrate creative works and works of the imagination. Although true crime is the primary focus of the Borowitz Collection, it also contains notable holdings in several other topics and genres, including a vast collection of sheet music spanning more than two centuries of popular musical taste and distinguished literary collections.

The collection provides rich sources to users as diverse as crime historians, film documentarians, museum curators, television and radio producers, antiquarian book dealers, novelists, and faculty and students of history, American studies, women's studies, and criminal justice, to name just a few. Kent State University is proud to steward this collection, and the present project to republish the Pinkerton detective stories is a further outgrowth of our desire to make these interesting and informative resources available to a wider audience.

CONTENTS.

———

CHAPTER XIV.

CHAPTER XV.

CHAPTER XVI.

CHAPTER XVII.

CHAPTER XVIII.

CHAPTER XIX.

CHAPTER XX.

PREFACE.

IN submitting to the public another volume of my detective experiences, I desire to reiterate the assertions contained in all previous works. The stories, as related by me, are essentially true; the incidents depicted have occurred, and the people of whom I treat, were, and many of them are, living men and women. It is only in the locality of the scenes enacted, and in the names, which I have given to the actors in these criminal dramas, that a variance with truth may be successfully alleged. In thus concealing the identity of those, whose crimes have brought them under the penalties of the law, I have been actuated by a sincere desire for their eventual reformation, and I have, therefore, withheld their real names, in order that no undue obstacles to that much desired reformation should be placed in their way.

In the " DOUBLE LIFE," I have endeavored to portray the strange career of a man, who for years moved in the best circles of society, who was universally respected, and regarded as a leading man in the community where he resided, and yet who was for years associated with hardened criminals, and actively engaged in criminal exploits. The life of this man affords a strangely sad study to the philosophic mind, and his final discovery and punishment is but the natural and inevitable result of evil deeds.

ALLAN PINKERTON.

PUBLISHER'S NOTE.

SINCE the following experiences were penned, their author has passed away from earth. After a long life of valuable service to the cause of honorable humanity, Allan Pinkerton, the great detective, has laid down the burden, and now rests from his labors. He died at his home in Chicago, on July 1, 1884, at the age of 65 years.

A DOUBLE LIFE.

CHAPTER I.

THE twenty-sixth day of July 186–, was one of the
most oppressively warm days that I remember to
have experienced. The atmosphere was heavy, the
burning rays of the sun reflected with intense power
from the white walls of the houses and from the white
stone sidewalks, poured down incessantly upon the weak
and sweltering community with a power that was truly
prostrating. About four o'clock in the afternoon, however, the wind suddenly veered around to the eastward,
and almost immediately afterwards the city was covered
with a dense black cloud, which completely obscured
the sun, and rendered gaslight a necessity. Soon the
air reverberated with a sharp peal of heavy thunder,

1

accompanied by a flash of lightning, startling in its vividness, then came the rain; a drenching deluge that threatened to submerge the city. Ever and anon the thunder rolled through the sky, the air seemed charged with electricity, and the lightning flashed at frequent intervals.

The scene was truly grand and awe-inspiring, and as I looked out from my office window at the warring elements, I could not fail but be deeply impressed with the grandeur of the scene, and my mind was filled with thoughts of the wonderful and marvelous operations of nature.

I had been considerably burdened during the day with a multitude of operations which required much consideration and prolific correspondence, and feeling exceedingly fatigued by the heat of the weather, I hailed with delight this sudden and invigorating change which had taken place.

My reveries were interrupted however by the entrance of a precocious messenger boy, whose rubber clothing was dripping with the rain, and who presented to me a dispatch.

Upon hastily removing the enclosure, I found the communication to be one informing me that the safe belonging to the Howard Express Company at Troyville, in Pennsylvania, had, three days previously, been broken into, and that the thieves had succeeded in carrying off nearly fifteen thousand dollars in money, and other valuables. The communication also requested my prompt attention to the matter.

The Howard Express Company, even at that time, was one of the leading forwarding agencies of the country. Their headquarters were in the city of Baltimore, Maryland, but their branch offices extended through the everal adjoining states. It was a branch and under the control of the great Adams Company, whose fame is world-wide, and whose agencies extend to every section of our great country.

I had previously been engaged in many important operations for this company, in which they had been primarily great sufferers, but in every instance thus far, I had been successful ultimately, not only in recovering nearly the whole amount of the stolen property, but in bringing the criminals who had despoiled them, to justice.

Upon the receipt of this message, I determined to commence operations at once. Delays are always dangerous, and therefore, notwithstanding the condition of the weather, and as there was an eastern bound train leaving Chicago that evening, I immediately dispatched my General Superintendent, George H. Bangs and four operatives to the scene of the robbery, with directions to examine carefully into every fact in relation to the matter and to leave no stone unturned in their efforts to ferret out the perpetrators of this crime, and to secure, if possible, the recovery of the stolen property.

Mr. Bangs at once left Chicago and in due time arrived at Troyville, where, in company with the men under his command, he took up his quarters at the hotel, and prepared for the investigation.

In order to avoid suspicion attaching to the men who accompanied him, they were directed to locate themselves at the various hotels in the place, and to carefully note the actions of any one they met, in order to discover, if possible, any person whose movements might excite suspicion and who would therefore require watching.

Having completed his preliminary arrangements, on the following morning Mr. Bangs sought and obtained an interview with the agent of the company, Mr. William Linwood, who was in charge of the office at the time of the occurrence, and who had first discovered the robbery on the morning succeeding.

Troyville is a beautiful, thriving little village, situate in the northern part of Pennsylvania, and contained, at this time, about twelve hundred inhabitants. It is built upon a slight elevation of ground, and commands a fair view of the surrounding country. Cedar Creek, a beautiful stream of water, runs through the extensive and highly cultivated farming district which lies beyond.

Here, from our point of observation, are spread before the view the well-tilled farms, with their capacious barns and out-buildings, which, with the neat farm-houses nestling beneath the sheltering branches of the grand old trees, form a picture of rural beauty and comfort scarcely excelled. Far away are seen the huge mountains, which seem to raise up their towering forms as an effectual barrier—not only before the vision, but to the extension of our knowledge of the world which lies beyond.

Not so, however, for the puffing of the locomotive and the clicking of the telegraph tell at once that Troy-ville is in direct communication with all the sections of our continent. Their merchants do a thriving business and various hotels afford accommodation to the numer-ous guests who make this place a favorite resort during the warm summer months.

The village is located upon the line of the Northern Central Railway, which affords an easy market for the disposition of the products of the soil, and for the busi-ness purposes of the town now rapidly growing in impor-tance and prosperity.

The citizens being, for the most part, industrious, easy-going people, were considerably shocked at the commission of this robbery in their midst, and were exceedingly anxious that the thieves should be caught and the money recovered.

The railway station in which the Express Office is established was situated about half a mile from the business portion of the town and was comparatively isolated from the surrounding houses, thus affording an excellent opportunity for the depredation, and insuring almost entire immunity from detection. There were no buildings within fifty rods of the depot, and as no watchman was employed to guard the premises at night, the operations of the thieves were, naturally, undiscovered, and their labors undisturbed until, upon opening the doors upon the following morning, the broken safe and disordered appearance of the interior awakened the astonished agent to a realizing sense of the proceedings of the night before.

He at once rushed out and gave the alarm, and since that time various efforts had been made to discover the perpetrators of the crime but without avail : so, finding their unskilled attempts at detection unsuccessful, I had been notified by the President of the Company, and requested to undertake the capture of the robbers.

Mr. Linwood, the gentleman in charge of the office at Troyville, occupied the dual position of station agent and agent for the Express Company, using the safe in his office as a repository for the express packages of value, and for the tickets, money and accounts of the railroad company.

Mr. Linwood was, to all appearances, a very honest, industrious man, and one against whom no suspicion could reasonably be formed, and subsequent events fully justified the belief in his innocence thus entertained. A few minutes conversation with him soon demonstrated the fact that he was entirely innocent of any connection with the matter whatever.

He related his story in a straightforward, intelligent manner, which, while it expressed his great anxiety about the unfortunate affair and his humiliation at its occurrence, at the same time gave no indication of a desire to conceal anything that would aid the officers in their search for the individuals who had so successfully possessed themselves of the property of the Express Company. On the contrary, he seemed most anxious for their apprehension.

From his statement it was learned that he had locked up the office securely on the evening previous to the robbery, and had gone home entirely unconscious of the state of affairs that would greet him upon the morrow. Inquiries soon developed the fact that he was a man who had, from his boyhood, conducted himself in an honorable, upright manner, and it seemed utterly impossible that, having reached the age of forty years, and all of them honorably spent in the locality in which he was at present engaged, he could have committed this crime.

Admitting all these facts as convincing proofs of the integrity of Mr. Linwood, the attention of Mr. Bangs was necessarily directed toward the discovery of other

parties, who might not be able to so successfully account
for themselves, in the matter now in hand.

The contents of the safe were ascertained to be :

Thirty U. S. $\frac{7}{30}$ Bonds . . . $50.00 each . . $1,500.00
                    (Nos. 163737 to 163766)
Ninety "   "   "   " . . . $100.00 each . . 9,000.00
                    (Nos. 259828 to 259917)
and money packages of various denomina-
        tions which aggregated to 4,500.00

which made the total loss to the company $15,000.00

A number of coupon tickets issued by the Railroad
Company were also taken.

Mr. Linwood further informed Mr. Bangs that two
suspicious persons had made their appearance in Troyville on the morning preceding the robbery and had
registered their names as

B. S. Davis and
G. Cromwell,

and from the account given of the actions of these men
there seemed to be but little doubt that they were the
robbers. They had left the town early on the morning
of the robbery, since which time nothing had been heard
from them.

It was further ascertained that no systematic endeav-
ors had been made to get upon the trail of these men, or

to follow them in order to learn of their movements, their manner of leaving, or their probable place of destination.

These meagre facts, as may be imagined, were not very assuring and afforded no favorable opportunity for a commencement of our labors, but as this was all the information that could be derived, we were forced to accept it for what value it possessed.

In order however to acquire fuller particulars of these men, Mr. Bangs returned to the Troyville House and requested an interview with the smiling faced landlord who appeared to be greatly interested in the affair, and who very cheerfully accorded all the information in his power to communicate.

As the men were entirely unknown to the citizens, it became necessary to obtain a more correct description of them than it had, as yet, been possible to secure, and after numerous inquiries the following facts were elicited which, in the absence of more particular information, were to form the ground work for our future action.

On the morning previous to the robbery, two men arrived at Troyville at about eight o'clock. They proceeded to a small hotel near the depot, and ordered their breakfast, saying at the time that they were drovers, and were going out into the country for the purpose of buying stock in that vicinity.

After having partaken of their breakfast, they went

immediately to the Troyville House and registered their
names as

$$\left. \begin{array}{l} \textit{B. S. Davis,} \\ \\ \textit{G. Cromwell,} \end{array} \right\} \text{ Worcester, Mass.}$$

They then went to a livery stable in the town and
obtained a horse and buggy, stating that they were
going to a town a few miles distant, and would return
in the afternoon. They did not, however, return until
about eleven o'clock at night, when they again put up
at the Troyville House. They appeared to be very rest-
less and uneasy, frequently talking together privately,
and excited considerable comment among the guests
and others who were seated about the Hotel. They
paid their bills before retiring for the night, and from
that time nothing further was seen or heard of them.
They disappeared during the night and in the morning
the robbery was discovered, and suspicion at once
attached to them.

On further investigation, Mr. Bangs was positive that
they had not taken their departure upon any of the
railroad trains leaving the place, and he resolved to
scour the country round about in order to discover some
traces of their flight.

The man called Davis appeared to have been about
thirty years of age, stoutly built, and about five feet

nine inches high. His hair was of a brownish color and rather short, and he wore dark full side whiskers.

Cromwell was about forty-five years of age, about five feet eleven inches high, slim build, dark complexion, dark hair and full beard.

A description of their dress was also obtained as nearly as could be remembered by those who had noticed them, and also the fact that they carried with them a black leather satchel which appeared to contain something much heavier than ordinary clothing.

An examination of the Express Office and safe disclosed the fact that the thieves had obtained an entrance by prying open the window of the building that overlooked the track, and that the safe had been opened by exploding powder which had been inserted into the key-hole. The safe was an old-fashioned one, and offered no very decided resistance to the efforts of the thieves, whoever they were, in effecting their desired object.

Further proof of this was adduced from a gentleman who resided in a dwelling, the nearest to the station, and who, upon the night of the robbery was awakened about two o'clock by the sudden illness of his wife. He distinctly remembered hearing at that time, a noise that resembled a smothered explosion, and the sound seemed to come from the direction of the depot. It seemed evident, therefore, that the thieves must have been

The Treasury Department was communicated with, and it was ascertained from them that the bonds having been intercepted and stolen on their passage to the parties to whom they were consigned, would be regarded by the Government as though they had never been issued by the United States, and that the secretary of the treasury had ordered the payment of the said bonds stopped should they be offered for that purpose. This fact was also mentioned in the circulars which I prepared.

The action of the Government in this matter materially lessened the amount of loss incurred by the Express Company, who are responsible to the parties who confide to them their goods and merchandise for the purpose of transportation, and who are required to indemnify all such parties for whatever loss may be sustained while said goods are in their charge.

Notwithstanding this fact the company were thoroughly in earnest in their desire to have these men brought to justice. They had been the victims at various times prior to this of robbers and thieves, and their only safety and security for the future, lay in making examples of the malefactors in order to deter others from attempting similar operations.

Our pursuit was therefore commenced and although its incipiency was clouded and obscured, the prosecution of our investigation developed a systematic course of crime, which, while it resulted unfortunately to the parties implicated, possessed many features that were at once interesting and romantic.

———•———

CHAPTER II.

Oaklands—The Scotch Farmer—Archibald MacDonald at Home.

IN the northwestern part of the state of Indiana, and about twelve miles from the shores of Lake Michigan lies the thriving village of Oaklands, immediately bordering a beautiful prairie, the soil of which is extremely rich and well-cultivated. The village is the center of an active and extensive trade. Various public institutions are located here and many of the residents of the village and surrounding country are possessed of a refinement and culture that is not often found in rural Western settlements.

The surface of the land extending for miles around is nearly level, or slightly undulating, until it reaches the hills of sand near the borders of the Lake, and enormous crops of wheat and hay are annually gathered which contribute materially to the enrichment of the agriculturist, and naturally, to the extension and improvement of the village.

Railroad facilities are abundant, and Oaklands bids fair, in a very few years, to rival in importance and trade many of the older towns in this wonderfully increasing Western country.

About ten years prior to the occurrence of the event related in the preceding chapter, there arrived at Oaklands a young man, apparently about thirty-five years of age, accompanied by his wife, a beautiful and interesting lady, and two children, a boy and a girl, whose ages were respectively ten and twelve years.

The gentleman, whose name was ascertained to be Archibald MacDonald, was a native of Scotland, who had left the country of his birth early in life, to seek his fortune in America. He had been for several years engaged in farming in the beautiful Chester Valley, in the state of Pennsylvania, and it was there that he had met the lady whom he afterwards married, and who was the daughter of a gentleman of prominence and of unquestioned respectability in the flourishing city which was in close proximity to the residence of young MacDonald. Being a man of considerable education, and evincing a refinement of manner which gave unmistakable evidence of the careful training of his youth, and being gifted with a handsome person and a captivating address, he won the affections of the young lady and they were married.

He cultivated the soil of the little farm which he had

2

purchased for several years, during which time the two children were born to them, and their life seemed to flow on peaceably and happily.

At length, however, he became possessed of a desire to go West. The glowing accounts which were frequently given of the wonderful growth of the Western world, and of the marvelous harvests which were annually gathered from the fertile soil, filled his mind with bright fancies of prospective wealth, before which his present position, though comparatively comfortable and prosperous, paled into insignificance. He resolved, therefore, to sell his little farm in Chester county and purchase a tract of land in the state of Indiana, where, upon a much larger scale, and with no greater expense he would be enabled to pursue more profitably the life of a farmer, which seemed to be congenial to him.

He accordingly came to Oaklands, and became the purchaser of a farm of five hundred acres of land, about three miles from the village, and at once commenced the erection of the buildings that would be necessary for the accommodation of his family, for the shelter of his animals and for the storing of the crops, which would surely be harvested under his energetic administration of affairs.

In all his arrangements he evinced a degree of good taste and judgment which immediately produced a favorable impression among the older inhabitants, and before he had settled upon his farm, he had made many warm friends and acquaintances among his neighbors, who greeted with cordial welcome the arrival of the pretty wife and interesting children who soon after came to take up their abode among them.

Archibald MacDonald at once bacame a man of prominence in the community. His knowledge of agriculture was thorough and extensive and his farm soon presented an appearance of thrift that was a sure indication of success. His stock was of the finest kind. The cattle and horses of the choicest breeds, all the modern improvements were utilized and he was recognized as a tiller of the soil who thoroughly understood his business.

Having brought his furniture from the East, his dwelling was furnished in a more luxurious and comfortable manner than any of those which surrounded him, and his children were carefully brought up under the tuition and guidance of their mother, who devoted herself to their education and improvement in the same thorough manner which had marked her own early days.

The husband appeared to be devotedly attached to his wife, and their residence upon the Western farm was fraught with as much happiness as they had experienced in the more closely populated country which they had left, and if the young wife occasionally longed for the associations of her girlhood days, and for the companionship of the friends of her youth, she never marred the peace and happiness of the household by any outward show of discontent or by a word uttered in complaint.

Thus the months and years rolled on and nothing occurred to interfere with the increasing wealth and popularity of the Scotch farmer. His children had now advanced to an age when it became necessary that their education should be extended. The mother's care must be relaxed, and they must be sent to educational institutions where more thorough lessons were to be taught and where a greater mental development was to be secured.

The son a handsome manly young lad of eighteen had early evinced a decided taste for the medical profession, and as there was an Academy for instruction in that particular branch of science in a neighboring city, Frank MacDonald left his home and began the study of the profession which he had chosen.

Kate, the daughter, now grown to a beautiful young lady of sixteen, was the beauty of the surrounding country. Her gentle manners and winning deportment had made her a general favorite with every one, both young and old, and she met with many a pleasant nod of recognition or word of greeting during her frequent rides about the country and visits to the village.

At this time it was decided by her parents that she should enjoy greater educational advantages than could be afforded at home and Kate was therefore sent to a select boarding school in a neighboring city where she would be able to acquire those accomplishments now considered so necessary to a young lady.

Mr. MacDonald had by this time attained a position in the community, of considerable influence. He was the leader in the various agricultural fairs that were held in this and the adjoining counties, and upon more than one occasion had successfully contended for the prizes that were offered as premiums for the display of fine cattle, for farm improvements or for the excellence and quantity of the products of the soil. He took an active part in the politics of the country and frequently interested himself in securing the election to office of the particular candidates of his choice.

His worldly affairs had prospered and he was everywhere recognized as a gentleman of wealth, of refinement and of influence.

With the increase of his possessions it frequently became necessary for him to be absent from home for several days, he alleging that his presence was required either in Chicago or Detroit. These visits were invariably made alone, but upon his return he would usually be accompanied by one or more gentlemen whom he introduced to his wife as gentlemen in business in one or the other of the two cities.

It was a noticeable thing however that Archibald MacDonald never made a confidant of any of his neighbors, nor had he cultivated any warm friendships among his associates. He tilled the soil and disposed of his harvests, he made his journeys abroad and returned, but with no one but his wife did he discuss any question which related to himself alone, either in a business or personal manner. He attended strictly to his own affairs and allowed every one around him the same high privilege.

Notwithstanding this he was very popular, and his opinions, given only when requested, were regarded as satisfactory and as convincing as though delivered by a judge upon the bench.

He was genial and hospitable, and the luxurious structure that now occupied the site of the unpretentious farm house of the days gone by, was more frequently visited than any other dwelling for miles around.

Perhaps, this consistent reticence on his part contributed in a greater degree to enhance his popularity than a contrary course would have produced, but certain it is, that no man in that section of the country was more highly regarded or more profoundly respected than Archibald MacDonald of Oaklands.

Craving the indulgence of the reader for this temporary digression, the full import of which will be discovered in the sequel, we will return to the town of Troyville, and follow the movements of my operatives in their search for the robbers of the safe belonging to the Express Company.

CHAPTER III.

Further   Investigations—A Torn Piece of Paper—A spurious Detective and how he was disposed of.

AFTER dispatching the men upon their various routes of travel, Mr. Bangs repaired again to the office of the Express Company in order to discover if possible any additional information that might be valuable in the further prosecution of this investigation.

Upon entering the depot he found Mr. Linwood engaged in conversation with a young man of rather doubtful appearance, who as Mr. Bangs approached them turned to him and extending his hand saluted him with :

"I suppose you are the gentleman who was sent for to come on and investigate the robbery."

Mr. Bangs imagining him to be an employee of the Company replied in the affirmative, when Mr. Linwood stepping forward, greeted Mr. Bangs and introducing him to the stranger, said :

"Mr. Bangs, this is Mr. Morton, a detective who has been engaged in looking after this affair previous to your coming."

"Yes sir," officiously broke in the young man, "and

I will be most happy to co-operate with you in the matter and furnish you with any information you desire."

This idea of co-operation was decidedly distasteful to Mr. Bangs. It is a fixed rule with me upon entering into an investigation to have the entire charge of the operation. The only co-operation I need is that of the men acting under my own immediate orders, and that has generally been found sufficient for my purposes.

Mr. Bangs therefore declined to consult with Mr. Morton, until ascertaining further about him and the nature of his appointment, and not being very favorably impressed with his appearance he resolved to dispense with his services as early as possible.

Mr. Morton shortly afterwards took his leave, informing Mr. Bangs that if he should desire his services he would find him at the Troyville House.

Mr. Bangs immediately telegraphed to the superintendent of the Express Company and requested the withdrawal of Mr. Morton, stating at the same time, that until that was done he could not proceed with that freedom which was necessary under the circumstances.

While seated at the desk of Mr. Linwood he noticed a portion of an envelope lying upon it. It appeared to be the remains of an enclosure which had been carelessly torn in half. He picked it up mechanically and read what was written upon it, which however afforded but

little information.   The words which yet remained
were :

$$\text{``}A. MacD$$
$$O\text{''}$$

and whatever the full address might have been he was
unable to tell, owing to the fact that the other end of
the envelope had been torn off at this point.

Mr. Linwood, noticing this action of Mr. Bangs,
stepped up to the desk, and taking the paper from his
hand, said :

"This paper I found upon the floor of the office
when I entered on the morning after the robbery.   I do
not suppose it is of any value, but I have retained it
ever since."

"If that is the case," replied Mr. Bangs, " I will
take charge of it.   It may be of no value or it may be
of considerable importance.   Events will determine that
fact, and I will keep it until it may be wanted."

What important events sometimes hang upon the
most trifling circumstances.   Neither of these men had
the slightest idea at that time that this little peice of
torn paper with the unsatisfactory writing upon it was
to perform a prominent part in the detection and punishment of the thieves who had committed this robbery.

Mr. Bangs carefully placed it in his pocket-book,
and patiently awaited a reply to his telegram.   In a

2*

short time it arrived, and it was to the effect that Mr. Linwood should at once notify Mr. Morton that his services were no longer required.

In company with Mr. Bangs, the express agent went to the Troyville House, and finding Mr. Morton in the reading-room, at once communicated to him the orders of the superintendent.

The embryo detective was diposed at first to dispute the authenticity of the communication, and to assert his intention to continue his work without heeding it in the least.

While he was expressing himself in a very forcible manner, Mr. Bangs suddenly remembered that he had seen this man before, and all the circumstances of that meeting were recalled as vividly as though they had occurred only the day previous.

Quietly tapping Mr. Morton upon the shoulder, he very good naturedly, but firmly, addressed him :

"Mr. Morton, if Mr. Linwood will excuse us, and you will walk up to my room, I think I can speedily convince you of the wisdom of withdrawing at once from this case."

Upon entering the room, Mr. Bangs closed the door, and then turning upon the excited would-be detective, he sternly said :

"Mr. Morton, you probably do not know that I am very well acquainted with you and your past history.

You have never seen me before, but I had the pleasure of seeing you, entirely unobserved, in the office of the Pittsburg, Fort Wayne and Chicago Railroad, when you were called up to explain the shortness of your accounts as a conductor upon that road."

The young man turned pale and his lips twitched nervously as he listened to this very unexpected recital from Mr. Bangs. He attempted at first to deny the charge, but he was soon convinced that such a course would not do.

"I will give you ten minutes to decide this question," said Mr. Bangs, "and if at the end of that time you persist in your present position, I will inform the Express Company of your antecedents, and the Railroad Company of your whereabouts. They may desire to know more about you than they have yet learned."

Morton, who found it impossible to pursue the course of denial he had attempted, very reluctantly concluded to yield to the demands of Mr. Bangs, and to leave the town that evening, which he did.

It was afterwards discovered that he had not been directly engaged by any officer of the Company, but that being in the Express Office at Elmira, in New York, when the news of the robbery reached there, Mr. Parker, the agent at that place, had suggested to him to go to Troyville and look over the ground.

He returned to Elmira and was paid for the time he

had been engaged, during which, it was learned, he had done nothing but swagger about Troyville, and relate gigantic stories of his wonderful adventures as a detective, all of which, it is needless to say, had no foundation in fact.

By my direction, Mr. Bangs induced the landlord of the Troyville House to allow him to cut from the register the two signatures which the suspected parties had written when engaging their rooms. These I immediately had photographed and furnished to my men, so that they might the more readily detect their handwriting should they meet with it in any other locality.

Having done all that was possible to be done, and having the field now to himself, Mr. Bangs established his headquarters in the city of Elmira, in New York, and awaited the reception of information from the men who had gone in search of the fugitives.

CHAPTER IV

A detective in Trouble—An angry Negress—The Trail Struck—Important information.

TO rely upon the memory of individuals in regard to events in which they are not directly interested, and which are of no importance to them, or to place implicit dependence upon their recollections of parties with whom they have had no previous acquaintance, and whose appearance is not calculated to attract much attention, is a proceeding which is sometimes associated with great danger and frequently leads to the reception of a vast amount of speculative information which is neither of value nor of interest.

This was, however, the only course left for us to adopt at the present time, and I felt confident that, notwithstanding the unreliability of the human memory, I would, by a rigid system of inquiry, arrive at sufficient information, which, although not in itself of a satisfactory nature, would enable me eventually to act intelligently and successfully in the case before us.

A rather ridiculous incident occurred during the progress of this inquiry, which, although reacting against the precipitancy of the operative, is perhaps worthy of relation at this time.

One of my men, William Louden, had been detailed to take the road leading directly west from Troyville, and he had made most diligent efforts to acquire some information about the fugitives, but without avail. He was about abandoning his present course, when on the third day, he discovered what he believed to be unquestionable indications that the parties he was in search of were in close proximity to him.

An old wood-cutter whom he encountered upon the road and questioned in regard to the suspected parties, informed the detective that two strange persons had for several days been occupying an old building in the woods about a mile from where they were then standing, which had been deserted for a long time previous, and that he believed they were still there.

The heart of the detective leaped within him, as he received this communication ; and as he thought of the imminent prospect of success before him, he determined to attempt their capture alone.

Fearing to reconnoitre the ground by daylight, he waited very impatiently until nightfall, when, bidding adieu to the garrulous woodcutter, he started upon his journey in search of the house in which, he had no doubt, the thieves had domiciled themselves.

Having definite directions as to its locality, he had no difficulty in finding the place, and upon reaching a convenient point of observation he dismounted, and took up a position which would enable him to discover, without fear of detection, whether the place was occupied or not.

Yes, there could be no doubt of that fact. His quick ear soon detected murmurs of subdued voices within the building, and told unmistakably of its occupancy. Quietly the detective drew nearer ; the voices became plainer, but he could distinguish nothing intelligible. His excitement became intense, but the necessity for caution was too apparent to permit of rashness. Already his mind was filled with enthusiasm and visions of a great victory filled his brain. Creeping quietly near to the building, he placed his hand upon the latch, and quickly throwing the door open he advanced into the room and presented himself, pistol in hand, before the astonished inmates.

Two frightened yells greeted the detective upon his entrance.

" Oh Lord, honey ! de debbil hab come, suah !" cried a voice, evidently that of a negro.

" Hab mercy, Mr. Debbil, we ain't dun nuffin," came from the female Ethiopian, as they both cowered upon the floor, at the feet of the wonder-stricken and disappointed detective.

Yes, Louden was a very much disappointed man, for instead of the thieves he had fully expected to capture, he had simply frightened two very excitable colored people, who mistook him for a representative of the evil one.

" What are you doing here ?" sternly inquired the detective.

" We ain't doin' nuffin, sah," answered the man, who was clad only in his pantaloons and shirt, " only me an Rosy was just gittin' ready fur to go to bed, when you flew in de door, and skeered de life outen us."

Rosy by this time had recovered herself as she saw that the intruder was human, and, woman-like, anger took the place of fear at once. She turned upon the detective.

" Wat am we doin' heah ?" she cried " wat's dat to you? Wat you doin' heah, sneakin' around de woods arter dark wid your pistol ? Me an' my ole man hab libbed in dis yah cabin jes one yeah, and we am goin' to stay heah as long as we like, and if you don't git outen dat door, me and my ole man will make it very warm for you, now I tell you !"

The impetuous detective had evidently made a great mistake, and he was very anxious to get out of it as best he could. He endeavored to speak, but the irate female was uncontrollable in her anger. Seizing a broom from the corner, she made a frantic dash at the operative, and before he quite realized where he was, he received a blow upon his cranium which convinced him that his Amazonian assailant was possessed of no mean amount of muscle.

"Dare now ! am you goin' ?" cried the negro, as she raised the broom for another blow.

"Yes, yes," replied the detective, retreating towards the door.

"Den go !" exclaimed the woman as the broom came down again.

But this time the detective was beyond the reach of this dangerous weapon in the hands of a woman. He had leaped backward out of harm's way, and as the broom cleared the empty air and found no object of resistance until it struck the floor, the force of the blow was sufficient to pitch the angry woman head over heels out of the door.

The operative did not await any further developments but took to his heels in good order, his last view of the deserted house being of a liberal display of the anatomy of his antagonist who lay sprawling in the doorway.

He had no doubt that he had been made the sport of the jocular woodcutter who had given him the information, and cursing his luck, and the whole family of woodcutters in general, he mounted his horse and rode to the next village, where he put up for the night.

Such experiences as these are, however, not very frequent, and even in this instance, a little caution and an intelligent preliminary examination would have prevented the occurrence of the scene which operated so decidedly to the discomfiture of the detective, who too credulously imagined that he already had fame within his grasp.

This incident did not stop our investigation in the manner originally commenced, however, and experience soon demonstrated the correctness, our preliminary investigation and brought to us convincing proof of the direction in which the men had traveled.

Mr. John Varian was an intelligent operative upon my force, and he had carried to successful conclusion several important operations while in my employ. To him had been delegated the northern route which led up into the State of New York. He had not traveled far upon his journey when he found sure indications of the fleeing men.

About five miles northward from Troyville he stopped at an hotel and inquiring of the lady who kept the house, she distinctly remembered two pedestrians who passed on the day succeeding the robbery; she also stated that they inquired the distance to the next town, and after drinking at the bar, they had departed in that direction.

Hastily dispatching his repast, the detective was again upon the road, and about six miles further on he discovered additional traces of the men. He immediately telegraphed his information to Mr. Bangs at Elmira, who directed him to proceed upon the road he had started upon, to lose no time, and to change his horse as often as was necessary, making arrangements at each place for the return of the animal previously engaged. Another operative was detailed to follow him up, in case there should be any opportunity afforded for the men to diverge from the regular road and take any other highway for their place of destination, which as yet could not be determined upon with any degree of certainty.

At a place called Mansfield they had remained over night and had left early in the morning. By this time two of the five days that had elapsed before starting the pursuit had been overcome, and the men, evidently imagining that they had eluded any one who might have been in search of them, were traveling at a slower rate of speed. They seemed to be making for the Canadian shore, and acting upon this idea Mr. Bangs directed John Varian to take the train for Buffalo and to search the hotel registers there for any signature that might resemble that of the two men who had remained that one night in Troyville, while the other operative was to continue his inquiries along the route.

While this was being done Mr. Bangs received a communication from Mr. Linwood, informing him that he had learned from a reliable source that one Frank Grant, who resided at Elmira, had been heard to say that if he chose he could tell who had committed the robbery, and requested Mr. Bangs to see this man and endeavor to interview him.

Mr. Bangs immediately instituted inquiries in reference to this Frank Grant, and soon learned that he was a man of pretty bad reputation and a "hard customer" generally. He also discovered that his assertions had been made in consequence of some disagreement which had occurred between him and the party whom he declared had committed the theft.

It was an easy matter to arrange an interview with this man, and in a very short time my General Superintendent and he were in close conversation. It was developed in the course of this interview that Grant knew very little of the movements of the man he suspected. His description, however, corresponded very nearly with that of one of the individuals who had been to Troyville, and Grant stated that his name was Vernon Barber. He had known Barber for about a year, and had first met him at St. Catharines, where he had gone to escape some difficulty which had befallen him, while acting as a substitute broker during the war—he, it is alleged, having entered into a combination with several men he had enlisted, to desert from the army after receiving their bounty; after which he would re-enlist them in different places. This plan had been carried on for some time without detection, until upon one of the men being caught, he divulged the whole proceedings, which being followed by a search, Mr. Barber had found it necessary to seek safety in flight.

Frank Grant further declared that Vernon Barber was an acknowledge thief, who had also been extensively engaged in horse stealing, and what made him suspect Barber of this crime, was the fact that he had left St. Catharines about the first of February, preceding, and coming to Elmira, had indulged in a protracted siege of intoxication, and that during one of his drunken conversations with a fellow-thief, he had overheard him say that he was going over to Troyville pretty soon, as he understood there was a pretty good safe there " to crack." This was all that he had heard, but being an enemy of Barber's, he had determined to put the detectives upon his track.

Of course this information was valuable, if true, and Mr. Bangs resolved to test the correctness of it at once, and as the two other men who had left Troyville to discover some traces of the retreating burglars, had not acquired any information concerning them, upon the route which they had taken, they were directed to repair to Elmira for further instructions.

CHAPTER V.

Horse Thieves at Oaklands—The Chase—And Disappointment.

A SHORT time after the departure of the children of Archibald MacDonald to pursue their education, the residents of the town of Oaklands and the surrounding country were thrown into a state of intense excitement which was as novel to them as the cause was vexatious to the parties interested.

Upon awakening one morning in June, several of the prominent men of the village and many of the farmers discovered to their dismay that their barns and stables had been broken into during the night and their valuable horses had been seemingly spirited away. The alarm spread instantly and soon the main street of the village was crowded with people the victims relating their losses in no very enviable mood and the listeners expressing their sympathy.

Among the most vehement was Archibald MacDonald. He too had been a sufferer, and a fine bay stallion of pure breed had disappeared with the others. He was loud in his denunciation of the thieves, and in expressing his determination to pursue them to the bitter end. A meeting was immediately called and he was unanimously elected as its chairman. On accepting the office he expressed himself in most decided terms against this outrage, and urged his neighbors to mount their horses at once and start in pursuit of the robbers who had so unceremoniously despoiled them of their property.

His words were loudly applauded, and his views were warmly received. Horse thieving in that section of the country was a rarity. Never before had such a thing occurred, and the residents were appalled at the manner in which this work had been accomplished. No stranger had been previously noticed about the village upon whom suspicion might fall. None of the hired men of any of the victims had disappeared and from this fact it seemed evident that a well posted gang of horse thieves had committed this outrage.

" We must commence pursuit at once," said Mr. MacDonald determinedly. "and therefore let every man mount his best horse and follow me."

There is nothing that the American people so much admire as a leader who is prompt, earnest and commanding. In society, in the church and in the councils of state there is always to be found one man, who by his energy of purpose by the exercise of a master will power, or by his promptness to command a situation that suddenly arises, at once steps to the front rank, and almost instinctively commands the action and the obedience of the men about him.

belonging to Mr. MacDonald, and as the one which had been stolen from his barn upon the night before. They were evidently upon the right track, and with a shout that awoke the echoes, they again pressed forward upon the chase. Their enthusiasm, however, began to fail them as they neared the shore of the Lake. Here they discovered the hoof prints of a number of horses that had been driven close together. A feeling of anxiety at once pervaded the minds of the entire party. Could the thieves have reached the Lake, and have embarked with their precious cargo safely and without molestation? It seemed to be so, and the hearts of the pursuers stood still with apprehension as they contemplated such a possibility.

"Gentlemen, I am afraid they have escaped us!" said Mr. MacDonald in a despondent tone, as this reflection occurred to him. "But we will pursue this trail to the end, and will not give up all hope until the last moment."

They rode on in silence but when they came to the shore of the Lake they found their worst fears realized. Here were the unmistakable indications of embarkation. The sand was torn up as though it had been trampled by a troop of horse, and it was very evident that the parties they were in search of had succeeded in getting on board of some boat, and had made their escape with their booty.

3

The broad expanse of water stretched before them and their pursuit was ended. The horsemen drew up in line upon the shore and gazed disconsolately out upon the broad surface of the lake. How beautifully the morning's sun danced and glistened upon the ripples of the water. The splashing of the tide at their feet made a music sweeter than that of man. The great rounding shores, with their hills of sand that surrounded them, seemed to be reflected with increased beauty within the limpid mirror which they bordered. Nature had prepared a glorious view, but not one of these men were in a mood to appreciate it.

"Gentlemen!" again broke in the voice of Mr. MacDonald, "our search in this manner ends here, but I do not yet despair of success. We will telegraph to all the towns around this part of the coast, and I have no doubt we shall soon receive some tidings of our stolen animals."

This course appeared to be the only proper one under the circumstances, and the men reluctantly turned their faces homeward.

Upon their return the suggestions of Mr. MacDonald were acted upon, and every device that could be imagined was put into practice, but from that day to this not one of the stolen horses ever found their way back to their victimized owners.

The promptness of Mr. MacDonald in this matter

CHAPTER VI.

*Kate at School—A Morning Walk—A Dangerous Encounter and
a Rescue—An Unexpected Meeting.*

THE seminary to which Kate MacDonald had been
sent, was an academy for young ladies of good
family and refined tastes. All the modern accomplishments were taught within its walls, and Kate soon became
a great favorite with her school mates and teachers, who
all yielded to the beautiful and gentle girl the homage
of their hearts. She was frequently invited by her
school friends who lived in the vicinity of the academy,
to spend the weekly recess at their homes, and it was
during one of these visits, that she became acquainted
with Clayton Wolford, a young and rising lawyer, who
was the brother of Kate's most intimate friend and
inseparable companion, Clara Wolford.

The home of the Wolfords was a large stone mansion,
which was lacated just outside of the city. The grounds
were most beautifully laid out, and the house luxuriously furnished. All that taste, refinement and wealth
could suggest, were here. The father, a genial, pleas_
ant-faced man, had amassed a fortune by the judicious

purchase of real estate, which had increased incredibly in value, was warmly attached to his children, and no expense was spared upon their education. Their mother was one of the most delightful old ladies imaginable, and her heart warmed toward Kate as to her own child.

Since their admission to the school, the friendship of these two girls had manifested itself in a remarkable degree. They conned their daily tasks together, and in the evening twilight would indulge in prolonged rambles, that were mutually interesting.

Of course, as these two girls were approaching that stage of womanhood, when thoughts of the opposite sex begin to stir their hearts, mutual thoughts were exchanged, and mutual confidences were indulged in. Clara had frequently extolled to her friend, the virtues and abilities of her handsome brother, who as yet, occupied the highest place in her sisterly affections, and Kate had been no less enthusiastic in her praises of Frank, her brother, who was pursuing his studies with a zeal that promised renown in the days to come.

It must be admitted, that both young ladies indulged in glowing descriptions of their respective brothers, and many a little romantic dream was indulged in during their quiet rambles—and the moon, which is said to have a strange and controlling effect upon the romantic side of human nature, must have oftentimes smiled cheerily, as these love dreams were related, and these momentous ideas of prospective affections were discussed.

Kate had become a frequent visitor at the home of Clara, but as yet had not been fortunate enough to meet the brother who was engaged in Chicago, in the practice of his profession, and whose visits to the old home were only made at long intervals, or upon some holiday occasion. It was not therefore, until the usual Thanksgiving party was given, at the residence of the Wolfords, that their introduction took place.

Kate, as was her custom, usually arose very early in the morning and indulged in a long walk before the hour for breakfasting arrived, and having come over the evening before, she had, as was her wont, arisen betimes, and, without disturbing any of the family, had departed from the house for her morning ramble.

The day was charming—the air was cool and invigorating—the leaves from the trees which were fast yielding to the cool winds of approaching winter, were scattered about the lawn which surrounded the house and along the sidewalks in prolific confusion. Kate walked lightly on, her mind filled with pleasing fancies and indulging in those vague dreams which sometimes occupy the thoughts of the young. Her life had thus far been a happy one indeed. Blessed with all the associations of a happy home, her childhood days had passed away in unalloyed pleasure. The idol of her parents, and the pride of her brother, she had never known a wish ungratified or a desire that was thwarted. Her school life—aside from the regrets at leaving home— had been exceedingly pleasant, and nothing had ever come to her to cause a moment's uneasiness or pain.

How could she feel else than happy upon this beautiful autumn morning ? Her eyes glistened and her cheeks flushed with that delicate rosy hue which a bracing atmosphere and a brisk exercise imparted. She almost felt as though she must give vent to her thoughts in song, to ease a heart that was overflowing with thankfulness and joy.

She had reached the outskirts of the city and was about to retrace her steps, when her ears were saluted with the notes of a ribald song, and shortly afterward an open carriage drawn by two spirited horses came dashing past.

The carriage contained four young men, genteelly dressed and who evidently belonged to good families, but it was also very evident that they had been engaged in dissipation the night before and that they still felt the influence of intoxication. They were no doubt returning from a night's debauch in which they had forgotten that they were gentlemen, and had yielded to the appetites of the animal.

As the carriage passed the young girl who avoided gazing upon them, one of the occupants called out :

"Hold on, Joyce ! I must speak to this little morning divinity."

With a loud laugh the carriage was stopped and a tall, handsome young man of about twenty-five sprang to the ground, and in a very unsteady manner approached Kate MacDonald, who had increased her pace to avoid the dreaded encounter.

"Hold on, my pretty maiden—do not be in such haste !" he cried, as he attempted to stop her progress by catching hold of the mantle which she wore.

Spurning the touch as she would the sting of an adder, Kate drew herself proudly up and faced the young man. How gloriously beautiful she looked as the dark eyes flashed with virtuous indignation and the cheeks grew crimson ! Even the drunken Adonis who stood before her momentarily quailed before the withering scorn of her glance.

"Come, come, my pretty vixen," he cried, quickly recovering himself, "this kind of thing won't do, you know"—and he again attempted to catch her by the arm.

"Unhand me, sir !" cried the girl in accents of anger, in which no trace of fear was evident. "You are a brave man to insult a lady in this manner"—then turning her flashing eyes upon the occupants of the carriage, she asked : "Will you gentlemen permit such conduct as this ? "

"An iron grip was fastened upon the collar of their drunken companion."

A loud drunken laugh was the only response from the companions of this man who were evidently enjoying the scene.

Their laugh ceased very suddenly, for a tall form stood before them, and ere they could realize what had happened an iron grip was fastened upon the collar of their drunken companion, and he was sprawling on his back upon the sidewalk.

"Harry Davis, you have strangely altered when you attack young ladies upon the roadway," and then turning to the others, he exclaimed "and you gentlemen are performing a noble duty in abetting such work! Joyce Allen, I scarcely expected this of you."

The man addressed as Harry Davis recovered his feet, and perhaps realizing his contemptible position at last, stammered a broken apology and walking toward the carriage when his companions silent and abashed assisted him to enter and they were soon driven away.

The eyes of the young girl were bathed in tears and her bosom heaved with suppressed emotion. Brave as a hero in the midst of danger, now that it was past her woman's nature asserted itself and the tears came in spite of her efforts to repress them.

"Pardon me, miss, but if you will permit me to recover my satchel and umbrella which I dropped a few steps back, I will be happy to escort you to your home," said the young man politely raising his hat as he addressed her.

After he had rejoined her, Kate expressed her thankfulness with all the earnestness of her impulsive nature, to which her companion replied :

"Indeed, my dear lady, I am only too happy to have been of service to you, and the only reason why I did not administer a severe castigation to your assailant was because I know him to be a gentleman of good family and an old friend. When he has sufficiently recovered from his folly, he will be as heartily ashamed of himself as you could wish, and I am sure this episode will prove a lesson that will not be forgotten. If you please we will now walk on."

Kate looked up with a grateful expression in her large dark eyes, as she accepted the offered courtesy.

She had no fear of this man. The dark blue eyes that were flashing with anger a moment ago, were bent in kindness upon her now, the voice that had spoken in stentorian tones of rage, were now modulated to the softness of a woman's, and as she walked beside him she felt that this was a man upon whom a woman could rely and whom she could trust to the end of time.

"I will not trouble you to accompany me all the distance," said Kate as they walked along, "my walk has been a long one, and you may desire to meet the friends whom you have no doubt come to visit."

"I too have some distance to go," replied the gentleman with a pleasant smile. "My parents live quite beyond the confines of the town."

"I," said Kate, "am temporarily stopping with the Walfords, whom perhaps you know."

The young man suddenly dropped his satchel upon the ground, and warmly clasping the hand of the young girl, in his impetuosity, exclaimed :

"Then you must be the Miss MacDonald of whom I have heard so much ?"

"Yes," replied Kate with a blush, "and you ?"

"Am Clayton Walford, Clara's brother."

Involuntarily their two hands clasped with a warmer pressure than mere civility dictated, their glances met in one long lingering look and in that look :

"They read life's meaning in each other's eyes."

Thus strangely these two had met, and as they gayly chatted together on that homeward walk, they little dreamed of the darkness and the storms through which they were both to pass in the years that were to come.

CHAPTER VII.

At St. Catharines—The fugitives within reach—A pursuit and an
unfortunate accident—A sudden disappearance.

MY operative John Varian, according to the instructions of Mr. Bangs, took the train for the city
of Buffalo, in New York, and arriving at the place in
due time, immediately began his investigations.

He diligently searched the various hotels, but failed
to discover any one that answered in the slightest degree
the description given of the two men at Troyville, and
an examination of the registers failed to disclose any
signatures that resembled either of those upon the books
of the Troyville House.

It was evident, from this fact, that the burglars had
not put up at any of the public houses in the city, even
if they had arrived thus far upon their journey, or were
traveling in this direction, and Varian was about giving
up any further search and awaiting developments, when
an idea occurred to him that was deemed worthy of consideration and adoption. It was barely possible that
the fugitives might have reached this city and being
fearful that detectives were upon their track, had

decided not to stop at any of the hotels but to push on their journey without hazardous delay.

Acting upon this suggestion, Varian procured a horse and buggy and drove out to the suburbs of the city, taking the main road leading northward. He had driven upon this road about six miles, when, noticing a roadside inn, he resolved to alight and make inquiries of the parties within for the information he was desirous of acquiring.

Here, to his surprise and gratification, he received undoubted tidings of the fugitives. The landlord of the inn distinctly remembered the two men, and his description of them tallied exactly with what had been previously learned regarding them, and they still retained possession of the black leather satchel, which it will be remembered, they were recognized as carrying away from Troyville. They had arrived at this inn at about six o'clock in the morning, two days prior to this, and after hastily refreshing themselves, had continued their journey.

Thus far our conjectures in regard to the course pursued by these men had been found to be correct, and we were, without doubt, upon their track. Unless they boarded a railway train, we were reasonably sure of overtaking them before long. It is true, they were still forty-eight hours in advance of us, and much might have occurred in that time to divert us from an intelligent pursuit, still I did not anticipate anything of that kind, and I resolved to push my inquiries as rapidly as possible.

It became necessary to anticipate, if possible, their reaching the Canadian boundaries, as I was afraid that if they succeeded in doing so, I might have serious difficulty in getting them away.

It will be borne in mind that I was not in possession of their true names, for I had no doubt that both B. S. Davis and G. Cromwell, given at Troyville, were fictitious, and I could not with any degree of certainty identify them sufficiently to procure the necessary papers for their arrest. It was, therefore, of the utmost importance that they should be prevented from leaving the United States.

Mr. Bangs immediately tranferred his headquarters to Buffalo, and the other men were directed to report to him there. Upon their arrival, they were at once dispatched to assist Varian in his search, and to report any discovery that might be made.

Leaving the two men in charge of the investigation, Varian determined to go without delay to St. Catharines, in order to ascertain whether the men had reached there, in case that place was the point of their journey.

Varian had previously been informed in regard to the suspicions attached to Vernon Barber, and upon arriving at St. Catharines, he began to make cautious inquiries for that individual, but without success. No one whom he met appeared to be acquainted with such a person, and he was reluctantly compelled to discontinue his investigations in that direction.

Entering a restaurant to procure some refreshment, he sat down at one of the tables, and having nothing to occupy his mind particularly now, he amused himself by studying the faces of those around him.

Presently two men entered, and taking seats in close proximity to him, indulged in conversation, while awaiting the preparation of the food which they had ordered.

Varian paid no attention to these men, and was quietly consuming his repast, when a familiar name struck upon his ear. These men were certainly talking of the very men he was in search of, and listening intently now, he was able to hear the conversation which ensued.

"I wonder what Vernon Barber was doing here last night?" inquired one of the men.

"I don't know," replied the other, "I did not see him, but heard to-day that he was here with a friend."

"You may depend upon it, he has been up to something lately," said the first speaker.

"I wouldn't wonder—who was with him?"

"I did not learn, but it was some Western chap, no one knew anything about him, and Vern. told the boys that if they heard any inquiries being made, they were to give no information about them at all."

Varian now understood why it was that he had gained no information in his previous investigation, and he listened eagerly to what was to follow.

"They left this morning early, and started in the direction of Port Dalhousie. It would not do for Barber to stay long in this place, you know—somebody might be looking for him."

Varian lost no time in finishing his meal, he had heard enough, and he must be on the road at once.

He procured a horse, and started upon the road to Port Dalhousie, where he arrived without having found any trace of the men whom he believed were almost within his grasp.

At this place, however, he learned of them. Some boatmen at the tavern on the lake shore had seen the the same two men pass eastwards towards Niagara.

Taking the lake road therefore, he hastened on, making inquiries at frequent intervals and occasionally receiving information of value. He pushed on as rapidly as possible, but his horse, a poor one at best, began to show signs of weakness. The day was warm and oppressive, and both horse and rider felt the effects of it, but he still kept on. When within a short distance of the town of Niagara, he saw on the road ahead of him two men walking very rapidly, and to his intense delight he noticed that one of them carried a satchel.

The heart of the detective gave a great leap as these

two men appeared before him. Fatigue was forgotten in the enthusiasm of the moment. After days of patient labor his efforts were about to be crowned with success—after a multitude of disappointments, victory was before him.

The men had evidently observed him and were quickening their pace, so striking his spurs into his horse he determined to overtake them.

How strange it is in this life of ours that disappointment crowds quickly upon the verge of success. How many times has the patient student after hours of toil and of privation—in the pursuit of science—when just upon the point of a fruition of his hopes, been stricken down by the hand of disease and has succumbed to the inevitable, leaving no history of the great discoveries he had made. How many times has the shipwrecked sailor, who has battled manfully against the angry seas and the storms and the tempest, when just within reach of the sheltering shore, fallen back weak and exhausted into the seething waves, through which he had fought his way with herculean strength, and has died almost within the arms of safety. How many times the skillful commander after a hard-fought battle, and when victory seemed about to perch upon his banners, has found some sudden and unforeseen circumstance occur, and has, in the midst of conquest, been compelled to suffer a defeat.

Thus it was with John Varian. The men were be-

fore him, and in a very short time he would be enabled
to determine the question of success, when his jaded
horse stumbled in the road, and falling suddenly upon
his knees, threw his rider over his head into the dust.

With smothered imprecations Varian raised himself
from the ground, and being unhurt himself, turned his
attention to the animal, who had also managed to regain
his feet, but who stood shivering with pain in the mid-
dle of the road.

To his intense chagrin he discovered that his horse
had lamed himself severely, by the fall, and that he would
be unable to proceed any further. Hastily leading the
animal to the side of the road, he fastened him to a tree
and started on foot in pursuit of the men in advance of
him. This accident had occasioned considerable delay,
but they were still in sight, and increasing his pace, he
commenced to run, hoping still to be able either to overtake them or to discover where they would take refuge.

The men proceeded rapidly along the path which
skirted the lake, until they reached the ferry, when
jumping into a boat which they appropriated without
authority, they rowed diligently away across the river,
and when John Varian reached the bank they had accomplished nearly half the distance to the opposite
shore.

In no enviable frame of mind did he contemplate
this operation of circumstances, but no time was to be

lost in idle complaining, or in unprofitable ejaculations, and he set about procuring a boat in order to continue his pursuit.

After some difficulty he succeeded in securing one, and as they pushed away from the shore, the other parties were just effecting a landing upon the other side. Under the promise of an extra fee, the boatman pulled lustily away at the oars, and in a short time the boat grated upon the sandy bottom of the river bank, and John Varian, throwing the boatman the amount of his fee, started off again in pursuit of the men who had so successfully eluded him.

No trace of them was to be seen. The earth seemed to have opened and swallowed them, or they had been spirited away by some unseen agency. Inquiries produced no information, and no one whom he accosted had seen the men or could tell anything about them.

The whistling of a locomotive, and the puffing of a railroad train, now fast disappearing in the distance, might account for their sudden and mysterious vanishing from view. It was barely possible, that they might have succeeded in reaching the train prior to its departure, and were now speeding away, exulting at their good fortune.

Varian at once telegraphed the result of his trip to Mr. Bangs, and also his suspicions that the men had taken the train, but fearing that he might be in error in regard to this, he determined to search along the shore, in hopes of finding some clue to the men, or if possible, identifying the boat in which they had made the journey. Mr. Bangs, immediately, upon the reception of the message from Varian, dispatched two men upon the road, and also telegraphed to all the stations, a description of the men, and instructions to detain them until they could be identified.

Varian continued his investigations along the shore among the boatmen, but gained nothing of any importance whatever. Nearly all the boatmen are more or less engaged in smuggling, and any inquiries are apt to put them upon their guard—consequently they knew nothing, or would say nothing about anything or anybody—and Varian finding it impossible to acquire any knowledge in this direction, was compelled to desist from this mode of procedure.

He therefore returned across the river to Niagara, and finding his lamed horse still tied to the tree where he had fastened him, he made arrangements for its return, and then going back to Youngstown, he took the train for Suspension Bridge.

CHAPTER VIII.

*Vernon Barber—A Sorrowful Story—A Woman's Love and a
Man's Betrayal—A Village Funeral.*

MR. BANGS meantime had made arrangements for
the discovery of the antecedents and whereabouts
of Vernon Barber about whom he had learned so much
from Frank Grant.

He ascertained that the family of Barber resided in
the vicinity of Rome, in the state of New York, and an
operative was directed to repair to that place and to
ascertain full particulars in relation to this man and his
family.

Arriving at Rome, operative Sully began in a cautious manner to obtain the information he desired. He
soon learned that a family by that name resided a short
distance out of town, but his informant could not say
with certainty whether they were still there or not.

As the afternoon was cool and pleasant and the journey not a long one, Sully decided to walk to the residence
of the alleged Mr. Barber and he set off at a slow pace in
the direction which had been pointed out to him.

He walked along whistling merrily, the leafy branches
of the trees by the roadside rustling pleasantly in the

wind, and the bright blue sky overhead unflecked by a single cloud.

As he walked along he came to one of those most lonely and desolate places in the world—a country grave-yard. Within its rude enclosure reposed the bodies of revolutionary sires and matrons, of the Mexican soldier and of the Union volunteer. Here side by side lay the village Squire and the village Tramp. High and low, rich and poor, all had found their final resting place in this quiet field where undisturbed by the whirl and cares of the bustling world they slept the sleep that knows no waking.

With his mind filled with solemn reflections the detective paused awhile before this "little city of the dead." As he stood quietly musing before a time-worn monument, and endeavored to trace the faint lettering of the inscription which told of the virtues of one deceased a century ago, he was interrupted by the rum-bling of carriage wheels, the tread of feet upon the gravelled walk, and the low moaning of a woman's voice that told of deep and abiding sorrow.

A funeral train, simple and unpretentious, was enter-ing at the gate. Silently and reverently the detective uncovered and remained standing until the little cortege had passed on to the open grave, newly dug, a short distance away from where he was standing.

Impelled by that curiosity which is invariably associated with such events, the detective followed the mournful procession and reaching the grave, remained to hear the concluding portion of the solemn ceremonies.

The simple rites were said, the trembling voice of the old Rector told in a few words the virtues of the deceased, and then amid the weeping of those gathered around, the body was lowered into the dark receptacle, and the earth fell with heavy thuds upon the lid of the coffin. The dead was buried and the living turned away to daily tasks in which they would soon forget the lump of clay which they had thus returned to its kindred dust.

As the coffin was being lowered, a shrill, heart-rending cry came from an aged lady, who was supported upon the arm of the officiating undertaker, but no other sound escaped those who had gathered about this last resting place for the dead.

Slowly the little group retraced their steps and the detective was left alone with a gentleman who had accompanied the funeral but who had lingered behind to give some directions to the men who were filling up the grave.

Thinking that perhaps this gentleman could inform him of the parties he was in search of, he approached him and respectfully inquired :

"Can you tell me, sir, if a person by the name of Vernon Barber resides in this vicinity ?"

The stranger started at these words as though he had

received a blow, and then turning suddenly upon the surprised detective, he asked:

"Do you know Vernon Barber?"

"No," replied the detective, "but I am anxious to gain some knowledge of him for a friend of mine, and if you are a friend of his perhaps you can oblige me."

"Friend of his!" exclaimed the other scornfully. "You might search this village through and you will not find one friend of his in all your journey."

"What has he done?" inquired the detective.

"Done!" replied his companion, "rather ask me what he has not done. Do you see that new-made grave yonder? Well, that is what he has done."

"What do you mean? He has not committed murder, has he?"

"I mean that he has committed murder. Not that he has taken the knife, the pistol or the poisonous cup to consummate his work, but murder has followed his actions as surely as though he had buried his hands in blood."

"Will you tell me the story?" inquired the detective, now thoroughly interested; and feeling that he could trust the man before him, he continued, "I am a detective, and am inquiring for Vernon Barber, who is suspected of a crime. If you have no objections, your recital may assist me in my search."

"Anything that will bring Vernon Barber to justice,

will be freely done by me," replied the other, in an excited manner. "I will tell you the story of that poor dead girl, whom we have just laid away to rest."

"Vernon Barber," began the stranger without further preface, "was born in this neighborhood, and as he grew up, his father, who was very wealthy, sent him away to school. But he was too wild and reckless to confine himself to his books and he was sent home. From that time he has never done any good whatever. Shortly after reaching his majority he went away from home, and nothing was heard from him until a little over a year ago, when he returned unexpectedly and remained until about three months since, when he as suddenly disappeared, saying that he was going west. We have heard nothing from him since, and his father has sold his farm and moved away."

"Then his parents are no longer here?"

"No, they have gone away. But to come to the story I started to tell you, and which has ended in that little grave and in a desolate home over yonder.

"Miriam Brandon was the beauty of the village, and the support of her widowed mother, whom you saw here to day. She taught school here, and every one who knew her had a kindly word for the pretty little schoolmistress. Many a young man had made advances, but none had succeeded in gaining the favor of the young lady, until Vernon Barber came home. His dash-

ing manners and handsome face, soon captivated the
demure and modest Miriam, and it was not long before
they were frequently seen together, walking in the evening twilight, or riding behind the beautiful pair of
bays which Vernon Barber had brought home with him.
Many an old dame shook her head sadly as she saw
this, for somehow or another Vernon Barber's manners
seemed to fill everybody with doubts of his sincerity.

" Several of her friends tried to remonstrate with
Miriam, but all to no effect. The gentle girl, in every
other matter so subdued, in this betrayed a spirit that
could not be controlled. She loved Vernon Barber with
all the intensity of her loving nature. He was her hero
and her God. What wonder then, that yielding to his
blandishments, she trusted to his honor and surrendered
her own to his keeping.

" A promise of marriage never intended to be kept,
an oath of affection as false as hell—and Miriam Brandon gave to Vernon Barber all that a woman holds dear
in this world, and became his wife in every other
respect except in name.

" Do not think that any one was cognizant of these
facts. Not even her aged mother dreamed for a moment of the state of affairs. Not the slightest breath of
doubt or suspicion ever clouded the fair name of the
pretty maiden who taught our school.

"Vernon Barber should have been proud of his conquest—he should have tenderly nursed that trusting love, which he had gained, and should have defended her until death, for the confidence she had reposed in him. But he soon began to tire of the lovely toy, and sharp words would bring the tears very often to the lovely eyes of the too trusting girl.

"Thus matters passed on, and at length a rumor reached the village that Vernon Barber was about to marry a lady from New York City, of great beauty and of princely fortune. The news came to Miriam's ears, and never doubting the honor of her lover, she refused to believe its truthfulness.

"Another fact became known to her. She was about to become a mother. All the love of her heart and all the trustfulness of her confiding nature went out to the father of her child. He could not be false. He loved her and she would believe in him.

"Poor girl, how cruelly she was deceived. Upon Barber's next visit to her, she laughingly told him the rumors that she had heard, and he, instead of denying them, affirmed their correctness. With a brutal sneer at her, he told her of the beauty and fortune of his prospective bride, and with an insolent allusion to her too confiding disposition he left her.

"From that day, Miriam Brandon never smiled again. She gave up her school and remained at home, and when, three months ago, Vernon Barber took his departure, she stood at the window and watched, with aching heart, his disappearing form, full knowing that she would never see him again in this world.

"No one knew of this, however, until one evening a few days ago, she called to her mother in accents of pain. The terrible secret could no longer be kept; the pangs of maternity were upon her and her story would soon become known to the little world around her.

"Then it was she told that heart-broken mother all the sad story. Her love, her confiding yielding, the lover's betrayal, and then, at last, a prayerful wish to die.

"Poor girl, her wish was granted, and to-day, sir, you saw consigned to the earth the body of the once beautiful Miriam Brandon, and in her arms lay the little babe that only once opened its bright blue eyes upon the scenes of earth. There they rest now, safe from harm, from calumny and dishonor; and Vernon Barber, whose dastardly deed has resulted in this sad work, will have much to answer for, ere his day is ended."

The detective listened sorrowfully to the narration of this affecting story, and as it was finished, he thanked the gentleman who had related it, and clasping his hand, he said:

"Rest assured, sir, that if retributive justice is a quality not quite extinct, Vernon Barber will meet the fate he so richly deserves."

CHAPTER IX.

The Men Found—and again Lost—Niagara Falls—An Unexpected Meeting—Another Piece of Torn Paper—The Detective on the Track.

WE will now return to the pursuit of the two men who had so successfully escaped from John Varian and who were believed to have taken the train southward from Youngstown.

It may seem very strange that after having reached the Canadian boundaries in safety they should have returned again to the United States, but I felt fully convinced that this divergence was only made in the hope of throwing any one who might be pursuing them off the track, and having reached the protecting shores of a foreign country, they imagined that pursuit, even should any be made, would then cease, and they would consequently be enabled to continue their journey unmolested and without fear of being discovered.

The unexpected appearance and desperate chase of the detective must have disturbed their plans very much and acted as a very decided wet blanket upon their hopes of having successfully eluded their pursuers.

That these were the men we were desirous of capturing there could be no doubt. Their appearance accorded entirely with the descriptions originally furnished, and their course from the commencement of their flight had been intelligently traced to this point. I was confident, therefore, that there could be no mistake about their identity.

My operatives had been started upon the road, and Mr. Bangs awaited the reception of some message which would inform him of the success or failure of their mission.

He was just about retiring for the night when a telegram was handed to him, and upon opening it, he found it to be from one of the men whom he had sent off that afternoon in the endeavor to intercept the supposed fugitives, and which read as follows :

" *Suspension Bridge.*"
"*Our goods here—come at once.*"

Ascertaining that the first train which would leave Bnffalo would not start until early in the morning, Mr. Bangs retired to his room, and after a light but refreshing slumber arose, and reaching the depot in good time, took passage for the suspension bridge.

Arriving there he met Operative Sugden, who had discovered what he believed to be undoubted traces of the men at an hotel there.

Upon the register of the hotel were two names evidently in the same handwriting as those which had been furnished him as copies of the signatures of the suspected parties at Troyville. The names upon the books were :

$$\left.\begin{array}{l} \textit{B. S. Henry,} \\ \textit{G. Carpenter,} \end{array}\right\} \textit{Tremont, Ohio.}$$

The names, it is true, were different from those originally given, but the initial letters were the same, and the formation of these letters were identical, consequently there could be but little doubt but that they were written by the same party.

The landlord, upon being interrogated, informed my man that these persons had arrived at the hotel early on the evening previous and had retired immediately after they had partaken of supper, since which time he had heard nothing from them.

His description of their personal appearance agreed perfectly with those already given, and Mr. Bangs felt sure that the game had been treed and would soon be safely bagged.

He posted Operative Sugden in such a position that he could command a full view of the door leading from the room occupied by the two men, and giving him strict instructions to maintain a close watch, he sat down to his breakfast with high hopes of immediate success filling his mind.

After waiting a considerable time and hearing no movement that would indicate that the occupants of the room were stirring. Sugden began to grow impatient, and procuring a chair, he mounted it, and turning the transom obtained a full view of the interior.

To his utter dismay and discomfiture he discovered that the room was unoccupied, the coverings upon the bed had not been disturbed, and the men had evidently not retired at all.

He immediately notified Mr. Bangs of this disappointing discovery and an examination of the room followed. The landlord was positive that the men had been assigned this apartment and the porter distinctly remembered showing them to this room which they entered and locked the door behind them, but the aggravating fact still remained that the birds had flown and had left no trace of their departure.

The hotel had been closed about one o'clock in the morning and the doors had all been found securely fastened when the house had again been opened for business and consequently they must have left before the hour of closing.

Every person about the premises was questioned, but not one of them had seen anything of them, their flight had been entirely unperceived and a private entrance upon the side street must have been chosen by them in leaving, as they could not have passed out through the main entrance unobserved.

The men were gone however, there could be no doubt

4*

of that. It really seemed as though the Fates had conspired against us and that we were to be continually doomed to disappointment just as we were upon the point of achieving success.

There was no help for it however, and idle complaints would avail us nothing in discovering their whereabouts.

One thing was evident even in the midst of disappointment, they certainly could not have taken any train at that hour, and must therefore have resumed their former mode of traveling on foot, and our search must be recommenced upon the same plan as that originally adopted.

It must be confessed that these continued disappointments had a very depressing effect upon our spirits. We had struggled bravely and manfully through the surging waters of speculation and theory. We had seen the alluring lights of a promised success shining brightly upon the opposite shore, with renewed energy we had redoubled our efforts, and then, just as we were about to realize that success for which we had been contending, our hands had relaxed and we had fallen back again into that sea of doubt, which we had so fondly hoped we had safely encompassed.

Notwithstanding this fact, however, neither our courage nor our energies failed us, we were still determined to succeed, and these primary disappointments instead of dampening the ardor of our pursuit, only served to strengthen our resolves, and to imbue us with a more resolute will to accomplish the purpose upon which we had originally engaged.

Recalling Varian and the other operative, who, together with Mr. Sugden, were soon closeted with Mr. Bangs, the orders were issued, and the three men, departing in different directions, began anew a system of inquiry, which, although not entirely successful thus far, had, at least, been instrumental in tracing the men to this hotel.

Much time had now elapsed and we were already far advanced into the month of August, ere these events had transpired.

Resolving to remain at this place during the day or until he heard from the men whom he had just detailed, Mr. Bangs strolled leisurely out to the famous bridge which spans the river at this point.

Walking out upon the shore of the river, he witnessed a scene never to be forgotten in the life of the tourist or the traveler.

Far away in the distance fell the roaring torrents of the wondrous falls, while before him were running with terrific velocity, the rapids. The waters from the great cataract, which rush to the bottom of the river above, and apparently disappear, leaving the stream unrippled and calm, here force their way again to the surface, and the dashing breakers rear their white crested forms high in air with a power and beauty unequalled in the world. The waves are lifted in wild fury many feet in the air, and then, sinking again, rush on to that circling vortex known as the whirlpool.

Nature, in all her beauty and awful grandeur, was spread before him, and after viewing the scene here presented, he determined to visit the wonderful and magnificent Falls, whose thunder could be distinctly heard, even at this distance. He therefore took passage in the little steamer that, during the seasonable weather, makes regular trips to the foot of the cataract, and from the deck of which, the finest view may be obtained of the falling waters.

After a short passage they arrived at their destination, and the glorious panorama, in all the fulness of its splendor, was before him.

No one can witness this great spectacle unmoved. An overwhelming sensation of awe and admiration at once takes possession of the mind. Hundreds of feet in the air rise the massive rocks, over which is precipitated the immense flood. The stupendous mass of the roaring and falling waters descending with overpowering force, dwarfs into insignificance surrounding objects, which, in themselves, are worthy of consideration. Before this spectacle, so sublime, surpassing, in majesty and grandeur and power, all the works of nature, the spectator becomes indifferent to everything else, and the mind is wholly absorbed in the contemplation of this miracle of natural grandeur which deserves to be classed as the eighth wonder of the world.

While Mr. Bangs stood wrapt in admiration of the beauty of the scene before him, his reverie was interrupted by a voice which he immediately recognized as belonging to Frank Grant, the young man who had given him the information about Vernon Barber, and had stated his belief that Barber was connected with the robbery.

"Mr. Bangs, good morning, Sir," said Grant, advancing, and extending his hand. "You have not succeeded in reaching Vernon Barber, yet, have you?'

"No, sir," replied Mr. Bangs, "but we are, I think, upon his track."

Frank Grant was accompanied by a friend, whom he introduced as James Cole, and who evinced a lively interest in the conversation.

"Vernon Barber!" said he, "why, if I am not mistaken, I saw him at the Great Western Depot this morning, in company with another man, and they took the train for the west."

"Are you sure of that?" eagerly inquired Mr. Bangs.

"Quite sure," replied the other. "I could not have been mistaken, as I have known him by sight for a long time."

This information had a very aggravating effect upon Mr. Bangs. There was no doubt that while he and Mr. Sugden were awaiting their appearance from their chamber at the hotel, these men were quietly taking their passage upon a train that would bear them far away.

Instantly the beauty of the scene faded from his view, the roaring torrents fell unnoticed, and he impatiently awaited the return of the boat, so that he might be enabled to prosecute his inquires in a manner that would convince him of the correctness of this information.

Concealing his annoyance and impatience, however, Mr. Bangs conversed pleasantly with these two men, and from their conversation obtained many important items of information of the antecedents of Vernon Barber.

Upon arriving at the hotel, the proprietor handed him a note, which he eagerly opened, and found to be a communication, which filled him with high hopes of success.

" *The two men took Great Western train for the west —will follow them and inform you of their destination.*
Sugden."

The operative had been in time to anticipate their departure, and was upon the train with them. This was good news, indeed, and Mr. Bangs immediately sat down and notified me of this favorable aspect of affairs.

Mr. Bangs again requested permission to examine the chamber occupied by the men upon the evening previous. Why he did so, he could not tell—there seemed to be some impelling force that led him to prefer this request, and he ascended the stairs, momentarily wondering at himself for this action.

Upon entering, the room presented the same appearance as it did upon his former visit, and there seemed to be nothing here that would add to his knowledge of its contents.

He walked mechanically to the window that overlooked the street, and gazed absently out at the passers by.

While standing thus, his attention was attracted by a piece of paper, which had been twisted and evidently used for the purpose of lighting a cigar or the gas—the end of the paper was partially burned, which was sufficient evidence of the use to which it had been applied.

As he untwisted it, however, he gave a start of surprise which so astonished the servant who accompanied him that he jumped backward in affright, evidently imagining that his curious visitor had gone mad.

It was no wonder that Mr. Bangs was startled, for as the folds and creases of the twisted piece of paper were smoothed out under his hand, he discovered that he had in his possession the other half of the torn envelope that he had found in the Express Office at Troyville.

Another torn piece of paper.

Hastily producing his pocketbook, he took out the fragment originally secured, and laying it beside the crumpled and burnt piece upon the table before him— the torn and irregular edges fitted together in a manner that left no room for further doubt.

The address thus completed, read as follows :

> "*A. MacDonald,*
>> *Oaklands,*
>>> *Indiana.*"

With trembling hands he replaced the two pieces of paper in his pocket, and for the first time since the investigation began, he saw his way clearly and definitely defined in the matter.

CHAPTER X.

Love's Young Dreams—A Brilliant Party—A Dangerous Ride and a Timely Rescue.

THE strange and unexpected meeting between Kate MacDonald and Clayton Wolford was productive of marked and pleasing results. Each had heard of the other quite frequently and in phrases the most flattering. Clara's love for her brother and her friend had induced a lavish use of compliments of one to the other, the effect of which had been to prepare them to a great extent for the acquaintance which had thus been made under such peculiar circumstances.

To Clayton Wolford the rare beauty of the blushing and indignant girl as she repulsed the advances of her inebriated assailant, was a revelation of loveliness which charmed every sense of his being. The proud poise of the noble head, the flashing of the beautiful dark eyes, and the clear ringing tones of her musical voice, made an impression upon his mind and heart that was destined to remain with him for a long time. Her entire absence of fear as she resented the attack upon her maiden purity and modesty, and the sudden transition to the womanly tears that fell from her lovely eyes as the danger was safely passed—all had endeared her to him in a manner that would perhaps have taken months of previous acquaintance and intercourse to accomplish. Already he began to experience that delightful sensation of which the poets have written and sung so sweetly since the earliest days of humanity.

Nor was Kate less susceptible than her gallant and manly rescuer. During her intercourse with Clara Wolford, she had frequently listened to the prases of her noble brother. Under the influences of these sisterly flatteries, Kate had almost instinctively pictured to herself in most luxurious coloring, the personal appearance and the manly virtues of the brother of her friend. Consequently when he appeared to her as the defender of her person, who had so herocially rushed to her rescue in a moment of, what she believed to be, supreme danger, she was disposed to regard him as fully worthy of all the encomiums which had been so generously bestowed upon him, by his fond and admiring sister.

Nor did his appearance belie his praises—tall and erect, with broad, firm-set shoulders, a finely formed head, surmounted by curling locks of chestnut-brown hair—he seemed fully to realize the dreams which she had so frequently indulged in. His dark-blue eyes, that seemed to twinkle so merrily with good humor one moment, and the next would be fixed with earnest gaze, upon the animated face upturned to his, gave ample indication that the heart of the man was true, and that his mind was pure.

It was not strange, therefore, that when they reached their residence, a feeling of mutual affection and trust had taken possession of them both, and that they conversed with the freedom of old friends.

As may be expected, their arrival together, was the occasion of great surprise, and explanations were a necessity, and in response to the eager questionings of the impulsive Clara, the story of their meeting, and the causes which led to it were fully disclosed to the listening family.

"It is too bad," exclaimed Clara, with an assumption of temper, which she was far from experiencing. "After I had planned the nicest little surprise for Clayton, that all my plans should be blown to the winds, and you two should meet under a veil of romance, that far exceeds anything I could have imagined."

"Never mind, Clara," replied the brother, laughingly. "Do not be angry, for you know that if I had not arrived in time, the consequences might have been very serious."

Kate blushed at the words of the young man, and with this explanation, the family passed into the breakfast room, where the morning repast awaited them.

Ah yes—their meeting had been a romantic one, but what shall we say of the events which were to follow !

That evening the Wolford mansion was in a blaze of light. The handsome parlors were brilliantly illuminated, and a large company of well dressed gentlemen and elegently attired ladies, were gathered together to partake of the hospitalities of their genial and liberal host, and to celebrate in an enjoyable manner, the Thanksgiving holiday.

Amid all the varieties of beauty and toilet, Kate MacDonald, was the acknowledged belle, and she was surrounded by an eager group of young gentlemen, all desirous of winning her favor, or securing her hand as a partner in the dance.

Clayton Wolford, as he looked at the beautiful girl, whose movements were so graceful, whose manner was so sprightly, and yet so modest, and whose toilet was a marvel of that quiet, elegant taste, which bespeaks the true lady, thought that he had never before met one who entirely fulfilled his ideal of a pure and lovely woman.

His attentions to the charming girl were much marked during the evening, and many of the ancient dames who had daughters of their own to marry, noticed with envious eyes the admiration which he so openly displayed for this friend and companion of his sister. Nor was the envy confined entirely to the mammas with marriageable daughters, for there were many young gentlemen present who would have given much for one of those bright ravishing smiles that invariably greeted Clayton Wolford as he approached the group which hovered about Kate when she was not engaged in dancing.

Frank and ingenuous in her disposition, she was entirely unused to the masks and disguises of fashionable society. She had never been taught to hide her feelings beneath the cold covering of indifference, and the enthusiasm with which she entered into the enjoyments of the evening while they proclaimed the novice, in no less a degree did they evince the freshness, the purity and the beauty of the child of nature, whose youthfulness had not been tainted by the follies, the vanities and the deceitfulness of the world of fashion.

The evening passed delightfully away, and as the last carriage drove off with the last lingering guests, Kate turned toward Mrs. Wolford and throwing her arms around the good old lady exclaimed with all the fervor of youthful exuberance :

" Thank you, Auntie Wolford, for one of the happiest evenings in my life."

"May you always be as happy as you have been to-night, my darling, for I am sure you deserve to be, and now good night, for you will want all your roses for to-morrow."

The next morning Kate appeared at the table as fresh and rosy as though the fatigues of the evening before had been entirely forgotten.

After the meal had been finished, Clara arose and addressing her brother said :

" Clayton, won't you take Kate and me out for a ride this morning? The air is delightful, and I know we will enjoy it."

" Certainly, my dear sister, nothing would give me greater pleasure, and if Miss MacDonald has no objection I will have the horses saddled at once."

Kate signified her pleasure at the invitation and soon the horses were champing their bits in front of the house awaiting the commands of the young people.

Clayton assisted the young ladies to mount, and then vaulting lightly into the saddle, the merry party proceeded gaily down the long sweeping avenue and out into the road that led to the open country beyond.

The horses were fine spirited animals and their graceful movements and proud carriage proved the purity of their breeding and the excellence of their condition.

The animal which carried Kate was a coal-black mare, whose very action was grace itself. She had not however been much exercised of late, and Clayton would have preferred the selection of some other, but Kate, who had ridden her before, pleadingly insisted upon riding her today, and all objections were silenced.

It was not without some apprehension that Clayton consented to this, but her appeal was irresistible, and he was compelled to yield to her request. He determined, however, to watch her every movement and to guard against any possible accident.

Kate's riding was simply superb. Accustomed from her infancy to the saddle, she rode with all the ease and grace of an empress. Her seat was firm, her hand steady, and she laughed lightly at the doubtful countenance of Clayton Wolford as they started off.

"Do not be alarmed, Mr. Wolford," said the girl. "I have ridden the Princess before, and I am not at all doubtful of her docility."

She did indeed manage the Princess admirably, and the noble animal seemed to be fully aware of the beauty which she carried. As they trotted along, chatting pleasantly, the fears of Clayton Wolford were dissipated, and he gave himself up to the enjoyment of the occasion.

The day was one of those that come bright, beautiful and sunny in the late fall. When the warm rays of the summer's sun seem to be contending with the cool winds that herald the approaching winter. The invigorating atmosphere soon communicated itself to the spirits of the trio of equestrians, and the sound of merry laughter was frequently borne upon the wind.

Clayton Wolford seemed to be in exuberant spirits. Never before had he so intensely enjoyed a gallop across the country, and if he had admired Kate upon their first meeting—if he had been impressed with her dazzling beauty as she stood in the full glare of the brilliantly lighted hall amid the throng of happy faces—he realized now that it was more than admiration which he felt for the lovely girl who sat her horse so gracefully, whose eyes were sparkling with merriment, and whose quick replies and merry humor evinced a happy disposition and a mind well stored.

Yes, Clayton Wolford was in love, and whether it was through the agency of his pretty sister or whether the inscrutable operations of fate had brought him to this state, he could not tell—he only knew that of all the women he had ever met the one beside him was the sweetest and most lovable in the world to him.

Never before had he exerted himself so much to be entertaining as during this delightful morning ride, and his conversation was of a character well calculated to produce a favorable impression upon his companion.

Thus they gayly cantered on until reaching the line of the railroad which crossed the road they were traveling. He cautioned the ladies to be careful as a sharp curve in the road would hide an approaching train from the view of the traveler until it was almost upon them, and serious danger might be the result.

Scarcely had the warning words issued from his lips than the shrill whistle of the locomotive was heard, and the flying train dashed by with lightning-like rapidity.

The horses started impulsively and affrightedly, and the Princess, whose conduct had been most exemplary heretofore, began to evince a spirit of restiveness that boded mischief. She reared herself suddenly upon her hind feet, and, turning swiftly around, plunged madly away in the direction in which they had come. So sudden and unexpected had been this action that no one was prepared for it, and the mare had cleared a considerable space before either of her two companions realized what had happened or were enabled to render any assistance.

The brave girl turned a shade paler as she realized the danger of her position, but with unflinching courage and firmness she attempted to guide and control the frightened animal.

All to no avail, however, so utterly overcome by fear was the Princess, that she became entirely unmanageable, and seizing the bit between her teeth, she kept on at breakneck speed, unmindful of the attempts of her fair rider, who vainly endeavored to control her.

Clayton Wolford soon succeeded in quieting his own horse, and bidding his sister remain where she was, or to follow him if she desired, he put spurs to his steed and was soon galloping in pursuit of the flying Princess and her precious burden, doubly precious now that danger was staring her in the face, and death, perhaps, was imminent.

On sped the wild horse, now utterly beyond all control, and it required all the presence of mind and firmness which Kate possessed to maintain her seat. Vainly she attempted to restrain the mad pace of the terrified animal, and at length, finding her efforts useless, with calm resignation and undiminished courage, she awaited with no little anxiety the fate which seemed to be in store.

On came the young man, the footfalls of his noble horse thundering upon the road behind her. One idea seemed to take possession of him, the safety of the girl before him, and he was determined to rescue her or to risk his own life in the attempt ; but his horse seemed unable to compete, in swiftness, with the Princess, to whom fright had given an added speed ; and his heart sank within him as he felt himself powerless to assist her.

Still he kept on, and at last he noticed, with a thrill of pleasure, that the leading horse began to lose ground, the lack of exercise had weakened her powers of endurance, and then his own began to gain slowly upon them. His exultation, however, was of short duration, for there occurred to him the dreadful thought that they were heading directly toward a swift running creek, whose precipitous banks rose several feet above the surface of the water, and he realized, with aching heart, that should he fail to overtake her before reaching there, the consequences to the girl he loved would be fatal.

Again he plied the spurs, and with a snort of pain, his horse dashed on at an increased rate of speed. Nearer they came to the danger that threatened them ; Kate, all unconscious of her impending fate, still engaged in the hitherto fruitless efforts to subdue the wild animal she rode, while Clayton, with his mind filled with terrible apprehensions, gave thought only to the doom which seemed to be inevitable, but which he was determined to avert.

Nearer and nearer they approached the fatal spot,

5

but nearer and nearer came the pursuing steed. Kate could hear the quick, labored breathing of the horse behind her, and then she saw the danger before her. She heard the firmly spoken, assuring words of the rider, and then she remembered nothing more.

When she recovered her consciousness, she was lying upon the soft grass by the roadside, her head supported on the breast of Clara Wolford, while Clayton, with tenderness and solicitude upon his face, was bending over her.

Two horses were standing near by, their quivering nostrils and heaving sides telling the story of the long chase, but the Princess was not one of them.

" Where am I ?" inquired the girl, with a shiver, as though awakening from a dreadful dream.

"You are quite safe now, dear, and all danger is over," replied Clara, soothingly.

She was quite conscious now, and upon being assisted to her feet, she discovered that she had entirely escaped injury. She looked thankfully up into Clayton Wolford's face, as tears of gratitude filled her eyes.

Eagerly looking around, she inquired :

"Where is the Princess ?"

" Come and see," said Clara, and taking the arm of her friend, they walked a distance of some thirty feet to the bank of the creek, and following the direction pointed out by Clara, the body of the dead horse met her view, as it lay at the bottom in the shallow and swiftly running water.

Silently she gazed upon the noble horse, whose career had been thus suddenly ended, and then she looked inquiringly into the eyes of the girl who stood before her.

"How is it ?" said she at last, "that the Princess is lying there dead, while I am alive and unhurt ?"

"You have had a very narrow escape, dear, and had Clayton been a moment later in reaching you, you might now be lying there too."

With trembling lips the fair girl related to her companion the manner of her escape. How as she fainted, and would have fallen from her horse, or been dragged to destruction, the strong arm of Clayton Wolford, who had succeeded in overtaking her, was thrown around her, and she was lifted in safety from the saddle. No power on earth could have stopped the speed of the animal she rode, and she plunged on, until, reaching the bank of the creek, she had leaped high in the air, and had fallen to the bottom and was killed.

It seemed almost a miracle, and it was only by the most wonderful exercise of strength and nerve, that Clayton Wolford had been enabled to turn his own horse, when within a few feet of the brink, and thus succeeded in saving his own life and hers.

A great shudder convulsed her frame, as she listened

to the story, but when she looked up at the young man's approach, there was in her eyes such a look of grateful affection and loving thankfulness, that many a man would have perilled his soul to obtain.

" My dear friend," at length said the girl, extending her hands toward her preserver. " How can I ever thank you ? You have saved me from a horrible death, and yet I cannot speak such words as would tell you of my gratitude."

Clayton took the two trembling hands within his own, and his voice faltered perceptibly as he answered :

" No words are necessary Miss MacDonald. To have been of service to you is of itself sufficient recompense. I only hope that no serious consequences may result from this unfortunate adventure."

They were not far from home, and Clayton placing Kate upon the horse which he had ridden, walked by her side, as they slowly wended their way to the residence they had left that morning in such gaiety and spirits.

But few words were exchanged upon the journey, but each heart was busy with its own emotions, and silence in such a moment was far more eloquent than language.

Again the intrepid young man had rendered valuable service to the beautiful girl, and each had learned in this second hour of danger how dear they were to each other.

Thus busied with their own thoughts the little party reached the home of the Wolfords, and it is not strange that as the young man assisted his fair charge to alight his hand should more tenderly clasp the delicate fingers which he held, or that the light of love in his eyes should be met by an answering beam from those of the rescued girl.

CHAPTER XI.

Escape of the Fugitives—My Operative Visits Archibald MacDonald—A Questionable Guest.

IMMEDIATELY after receiving the message from Operative Sugden, Mr. Bangs informed me of the progress that had thus far been made in the matter, and of the important discovery of the balance of the directed envelope found in the Express Office at Troyville.

I therefore lost no time in perfecting a plan of operations that would at once determine the question whether the information thus received was of value or otherwise.

It was barely possible that the person to whom the envelope had belonged, and who had so carelessly disposed of it, might be one who had business dealings with the gentleman whose name was indorsed upon it ;

it might be that the identification of the person thus addressed would lead to the discovery of the real criminal, or it might eventually transpire that neither the two scraps of paper and the name indorsed upon it would be of any practical value whatever in the investigation.

Whatever the result might be, however, it became a matter of the utmost necessity to trace the individual whose name was upon the paper, and whom, up to this time, I had never seen nor heard of. I was impressed with the idea that in some manner this Archibald Mac-Donald was to bear an important relation to the matter now in hand, and I resolved to cultivate his acquaintance without delay, if he could be found.

Whatever hopes were entertained of our being upon the track of the fugitives were soon dissipated, and again Fate intervened between us and success.

Sugden, the operative who had succeeded in boarding the train upon which the supposed thieves had taken passage, and who was entirely unknown to them, entered the car and took a seat where he would be enabled to watch their movements unobserved.

Upon making a closer examination of their persons than he had as yet had an opportunity of doing, he became convinced that both men were disguised ; that their hair and whiskers were not of a natural color, and that some material had been used upon their faces that would change their complexions, for both men appeared to be as swarthy as Indians.

Nothing occurred upon the journey of any moment and the detective was congratulating himself upon the fact that he would soon be able to determine their stopping place and to report the fact that they had been successfully located. During all the time he managed to keep them ever in sight, but this indeed was no serious task, for the men moved about but little, and seemed to be taking their traveling experience in a very matter of fact sort of way.

The train at length reached Detroit, and as the men prepared to leave the car the detective quietly and unobservedly followed them, supposing that they had reached their destination and that he was upon the eve of discovering their place of abode.

This proved to be a mistake, however, for the men simply walked into the refreshment room and seated themselves for supper, the detective within easy distance. Finding the men thus unconcernedly awaiting their repast, Sugden went over to the telegraph office and forwarded a dispatch to Mr. Bangs, informing him of the result of his mission and that the men were still with him.

Having performed this task he returned to the refreshment room and prepared to resume his duty of watching.

What was his dismay, however, to find that the men whom he had so zealously guarded had disappeared, and no trace of them was to be discovered. They had not stopped to partake of their repast, but had evidently departed hurriedly, whether being called suddenly away or whether they had grown suspicious of the detective and had seized the moment of his temporary absence for their departure he could not tell.

He only knew that the men were gone.

No time was now to be lost, and he hurriedly inquired of the waiters, but none of them remembered having seen anything of the parties—waiters never do— and the cashier only recollected that two men, as described, had paid for their suppers and had gone out. He hastened to the train, and quickly boarding it, searched every car, but no one at all resembling the men he was after did he find. Their disappearance was sure, and not a trace was left of their whereabouts. The detective stood utterly dumbfounded at the unexpected turn which affairs had taken, and completely discomfited at the failure of his dream.

From the topmost pinnacle of fancied success he had been hurled to the depths of acknowledged and vexatious defeat.

Another examination of the train and a careful survey of all the persons assembled about the depot only confirmed the aggravating fact that the birds had flown, and that their flight was a mystery he could not fathom. There was no help for it, however, and soon the information of his unforeseen misfortune was following the congratulatory message, the sending of which had occasioned this dilemma.

As the men were not upon the train, he determined to remain in the city of Detroit and to watch carefully for them, in the hope that they would remain here and that he might accidentally encounter them. As the train was about to move off, he again went through the cars, and again without success—the men he was in search of were not on board, and his westward journey also ended here.

Upon being informed of this unfortunate result to my operative I was, as might be expected, much disappointed and chagrined. I could not however accuse the man of carelessness, for it was his duty to telegraph his progress, and he had every reason to imagine that when two men sit down to a table and order a repast they will remain long enough to consume it. I could only regard it as one of those unfortunate operations of circumstances which frequently occur and which are none the less annoying because they cannot be logically accounted for.

The only thing that now remained for us was to make the effort to discover the Archibald MacMonald, whose residence was at Oaklands, and whose name was upon the mysterious pieces of envelope now in our possession.

I therefore dispatched a reliable operative to the place above named, with instructions to discover this person and to learn the full particulars of his history, his mode of living and any facts in relation to his movements that might be of service to us.

Entering Oaklands as the agent of a manufacturer of farming implements, the operative was soon enabled to make the acquaintance of the prominent men of business in the town and of the principal farmers in the neighborhood. By judicious inquiries he soon learned the history of Archibald MacDonald which has thus far been detailed by me.

Archibald MacDonald was at home when my operative reached the town, he having returned from a business trip, as was stated, to Chicago, and after establishing his headquarters at the principal store, my operative procured a horse and buggy and drove out to the house of the Scottish farmer.

As he approached the place he was particularly impressed with the high order of cultivation which was everywhere apparent. The fences which enclosed the broad acres were in excellent condition and the waving fields of grain that grew upon the soil were very luxuriant. As he drew near to the residence of the Western farmer, he noticed the large and commodious house in which he resided with his family when at home, but which family now consisted only of himself and wife, the son and daughter being away from home pursuing their studies as has already been stated.

The dwelling was a large, square one story structure with wide doorways and high windows which opened upon the portico that entirely surrounded the house. A broad flight of steps led up to the main entrance, and this was approached by a winding driving avenue which bordered by brilliant flowers of various hues. A sloping and undulating lawn of several acres surrounded the house, which, with its closely cut grass and numerous ornamental beds of flowering plants added a graceful charm to the rural beauty of the place. Large numbers of rare evergreens and choice perennials raised their forms and waved their branches in the wind. Everything presented to the view denoted the presence of an exalted taste and a neatness and beauty which at once proclaimed it to be the home of a happy and contented family.

The outbuildings also displayed the same degree of strength, beauty and durability which marked the home. It seemed to the detective, as he turned his horse into the winding avenue and approached the house that Archibald MacDonald must be a very happy man, and that his life was more than pleasantly spent. He could scarcely repress a feeling of envy, as he contrasted

the beauty which surrounded him, to the many change-
ful and vicarious scenes through which he had passed in
his life, while engaged in the pursuit of criminals, and
in the interest of justice.

Ascending the broad stairway, he rang the bell,
which was answered by a neatly dressed chambermaid,
to whom he handed his business card, and requested to
see the owner of the premises.

He was ushered into a broad passage-way, which
extended the entire length of the building, and which
was furnished as luxuriously as many drawing rooms.

" Mr. MacDonald is in the library, and I will inquire
if he will see you. He has just returned from Chicago,
and is very busy," said the girl, in answer to his question.

She returned in a few moments, and stated that Mr.
MacDonald would see him as soon as he had dispatched
a visitor with whom he was at present engaged.

After a short time had elapsed, during which the
detective had improved his opportunity to make a
minute examination of the premises, he was requested
to walk into the library, where the proprietor of the
farm was prepared to receive him.

The room into which he was now conducted, was a
large square apartment, handsomely furnished, and
tighted by two large windows, which opened upon the
portico, and through which, the cool morning breeze was
blowing. Arranged around the walls, were several

small book cases, well filled with their literary treasures, and at a table in the centre of the room, surrounded by a number of books and papers, sat Archibald MacDonald.

He arose to greet the detective as he entered, and as he did so, my operative was enabled to obtain a full view of his person. He was tall and spare, with broad shoulders, and a lithe elastic frame. His hair, which was of a light flaxen color, was brushed carelessly from his high forehead, beneath which, his smoothly shaven face, and clear cut, rather handsome features, appeared in full relief. He was apparently a man about forty-five years of age, and though slightly sunburned from exposure to the weather, his complexion was as fresh as that of a boy.

With an ease of manner, which bespoke the gentility of his early breeding, he greeted the new-comer, and requested him to be seated.

Upon stating the nature of his business, he was gratified to learn that Mr. MacDonald was in need of some agricultural implements, among which was a reaping machine of modern invention.

While engaged thus in conversation a gentleman entered the room from the portico and through the window, and as Mr. MacDonald looked up when he made his appearance the detective's quick eye noticed that a shade of annoyance passed over his face.

No words were exchanged, however, and the stranger selecting a book from one of the shelves again left the room as he had entered it, by the window, and the conversation was again resumed.

My operative with an assumption of knowledge of the subject of his visit, and by the aid of illustrated catalogues, had succeeded in impressing Mr. MacDonald with the merits of a particular machine.

"My only difficulty," said Mr. MacDonald, "is that I am afraid none of my men will perfectly understand the workings of your reaper, and I may experience considerable trouble in operating it."

"That can very easily be overcome," replied the detective. "We can send a man with the machine, who will put it together and will cut your grain, and by that means will be able to instruct any man whom you may desire to acquire such knowledge."

After some further conversation upon the subject the detective arose to go, and Mr. MacDonald accompanied him to the door. As they reached the portico, the person who had entered the library while they were conversing was discovered seated near the door reading.

This person was a young man apparently thirty-five years of age, of medium height, and with a smooth face and rather handsome features ; his complexion was clear and bright, and his dark hair was cut close to his well formed head.

As the detective bade Mr. MacDonald good morning
and decended the steps, that gentleman turned toward
the reader, and addressing him in terms loud enough to
be heard by the detective, said:

"Well, Barber, how do you think the farm has improved since you were here last?"

The reply of the individual addressed was inaudible
to the detective, but the name of Barber was instantly
fastened upon his mind and I was very soon informed
of this important discovery.

Here, then, was some chain of proof which could be
followed to advantage. If Vernon Barber was the thief
it was certain that his whereabouts were known, and the
opportunity of watching him was now afforded.

His intimacy with a gentleman of the acknowledged
respectability of Mr. Archibald MacDonald was a matter
of curious speculation with me. It seemed impossible
that he would be admitted as a guest at this house if
the owner was aware of the true character of the man
he was entertaining, and yet there must be an intimacy
of a friendly nature between them, and they must have
maintained a correspondence with each other, else how
could this man Barber have had in his possession a
letter addressed to Archibald MacDonald?

The general character of Mr. MacDonald, so far as
could be ascertained through the inquiries of my operative, was of such eminent respectability, that I was at

first utterly at a loss to account for the intimacy which seemed to exist between him and one who in his own native town, bore such a bad reputation.

However, I resolved to probe the matter to the bottom, and having an extensive acquaintance among all of the most prominent business men in Chicago, I had no difficulty in procuring the machine desired by the farmer, and of forwarding it to him.

All the other men engaged upon this operation were relieved, and I determined to pursue this branch of the investigation only.

I had upon my force at the time, a young and intelligent operative by the name of Henry Pinkham. He was an excellent mimic, and with a fund of anecdote that was quite wonderful. Almost every incident that occurred under his notice, served as a reminder of something which he had heard previously, and which would afford an opportunity for the relation of some interesting story apropos to the occasion.

He was a fine looking young fellow, with a frank open expression of countenance, that invariably won the favor of those with whom he came in contact. He was also very easy and gentlemanly in his manner and deportment, and was perfectly at home in any society.

A very little instruction was necessary to educate him in the management of the new machine, and as he had been reared upon a farm, his early training stood him in good stead in this instance, and I at once selected him for the purpose of the present investigation.

Giving him full and explicit directions as to the nature of the operation, and with strict orders to furnish me with full and prompt reports of whatever occurred under his notice, he was dispatched to Oaklands, with what result, will hereafter be shown.

———◆———

CHAPTER XII.

The Detective Domiciled at Oaklands—He hears something of Importance.

IT was a beautiful morning when Henry Pinkham arrived at Oaklands. A refreshing shower of rain had fallen during the night, and under the beams of the morning's sun, the grass and trees bloomed forth with a freshness and beauty that charmed the eye and delighted the senses.

As he stood upon the platform after leaving the train, Mr. MacDonald approached and in his usual gracious manner addressed him.

"Are you the young man, sir, who was to accompany a reaping machine consigned to Archibald MacDonald ?"

"I am, sir," replied Pinkham, "and I presume you are that gentleman."

"Yes, sir," was the reply, "and if you will step this way, Mr. Pinkham, I will drive you over to the farm.'

Upon reaching the carriage, which was waiting at the other end of the depot, the man designated as Vernon Barber was found seated therein, and conversing pleasantly with the express agent, who was upon the platform.

"Step right in, Mr. Pinkham," said Mr. MacDonald, "you have arrived just in time, as I think we shall commence cutting our grain to-morrow. Mr. Barber, this is the young man who is to operate upon the new reaper which I have purchased."

Vernon Barber acknowledged the salutation, and as he looked up into the face of the man before him, the detective imagined that he saw a resemblance to some one he had seen before. Despite his present absence of whiskers, there was something about the appearance of Vernon Barber which awoke some latent memories, but which were too vague and too unsatisfactory at present to afford him any relief. Without troubling himself, however, about this, he stepped into the carriage and they were soon speeding along the road towards the farm.

Between Archibald MacDonald and his guest there seemed to exist a mutual interest and of a business nature, and their manner towards each other was quite friendly. Now and then, however, the detective would notice a quick cloud pass over the countenance of the elder of the two men, and for a moment or two he would appear to be ill at ease and annoyed.

As they rode along, Barber turned towards his host and said :

"The races are to come off in Chicago next Thursday, shall you go over ?"

"I don't know," replied MacDonald, " I should like to see them very much, and if I can arrange my affairs, I think I will go."

They drove into the winding avenue as he spoke, and the conversation upon that subject was dropped as they espied Mrs. MacDonald approaching them through the shrubbery.

Mrs. MacDonald was a very beautiful woman, even at her age, and it was from her that Kate had inherited the large lustrous dark eyes which lighted up her face so magically.

The husband drew up beside her as she neared them and introduced Pinkham, whom he desired should be accommodated at the farm house during the time that he remained.

The wife with a graceful courtesy acknowledged the polite salutation of the young detective, and the three men alighting, the horses were led around to the barn by a black boy who stood near, awaiting their arrival.

Pinkham thus became pleasantly domiciled at the

residence of Archibald MacDonald, and he resolved to cultivate the acquaintance of Vernon Barber at once.

During the day he went over the fields that were to be harvested on the morrow, and with the assistance of one of the men upon the farm the new machine was put together and was ready for use.

The conduct of Pinkham at once won for him the favor of those around him, and at nightfall when the evening repast was over and the family had gathered in the library room, his pleasing stories proved quite a source of entertainment.

Just before retiring for the night Mr. MacDonald as was his custom when at home paid a visit to the barns and outbuildings to see that everything was properly arranged for the night. Inviting Pinkham to accompany him, the two started out, and with the watchful care of a good master, he saw that the stock was properly provided for, and then returned to the house.

"I am afraid, Mr. Pinkham, we shall not be able to do any harvesting to-morrow; the weather looks very threatening and I fear we shall have rain."

Pinkham felt quite satisfied at this prospect; for the longer the delay, the better opportunity he would have of cultivating the suspicious visitor at the Oaklands farm.

True enough, early on the following day, the gathering clouds broke over their heads, and the rain, a heavy, regular pour came down with a steadiness that promised long continuance, and labor in the fields was postponed for that day.

Pinkham having nothing particular to attract his attention or to which he could devote his mind, walked into the library and selecting a book seated himself within one of the large curtained window and began to read.

He had not been thus employed very long when Vernon Barber accompanied by Mr. MacDonald entered the room and seated themselves at the table.

"This cold wet day is enough to chill one to the bone, Mack," said Barber, with an easy air of familiarity. "Where is your spirit bottle, I think I will take a drink?"

The bottle and glasses were produced, and the two gentlemen partook of a liberal potation with evident relish.

"What do you think of going to the races on Thursday?" inquired Barber.

"I do not know yet, but to-morrow I will decide whether I will go or not," replied MacDonald.

"We may be able to meet some one there who will be of service to us, and as we must be very careful in this matter, it is necessary that we should engage some shrewd party."

"Barber, I don't like this business at all, and I wish we had never engaged in it. There is danger ahead, I am sure, and if my wife or children should suffer through any act of mine, I should go mad."

"Nonsense, old man, there is not a particle of danger, and you are fretting yourself for nothing," cheerily responded the other. "All we have to do, is to place the matter in the hands of some reliable party, and the work is done."

"Barber, I tell you I don't like it. I have never felt comfortable since we began it. I am not superstitious, but I cannot escape the ever present fear that trouble will grow out of it."

"Don't be foolish, Mack. You know as well as I do, that we are perfectly safe in this arrangement, and that nobody will be hurt by what is done. Why then, do you continually worry about unnecessary trifles?"

The detective had thus far not been observed, the heavy folds of the curtain completely hiding him from view, and keeping perfectly quiet, he listened intently to the conversation that was taking place.

What business arrangements could these two men have in common with each other? And by what right of association did Vernon Barber thus so familiarly address his companion?

These questions flitted confusedly through the mind of the detective, but with the present lights before him, no satisfactory solution of the problem was afforded. It was evident, however, that there was a well understood interest in which they participated in common, and what it was, he resolved to ascertain.

"Perhaps it is foolish and weak, but I cannot evade the feelings that I experience in regard to it," replied Mr. MacDonald.

Barber laughed lightly, and rising to his feet, he came over to his friend, and tapping him upon the shoulder, said :

"Now old boy, don't be womanish. I think I will take a walk around the barn and smoke a cigar. Now don't think any more about it, and while I am gone, do you try to make up your mind to go to Chicago on Thursday."

Saying which, he filled himself another glass of liquor, walked carelessly out of the room, and went down the lane toward the barn.

Mr. MacDonald sat buried in deep thought for some time after the departure of his friend. At length he arose, and walking toward a secretary that stood against the wall opposite to the window at which the detective was seated, he opened it, and taking out a small square metallic box, he unlocked it and raised the lid.

Silently he stood gazing at its contents, and then shaking his head sadly, he murmured to himself, but quite audibly to the detective :

"Are these things worth a man's honor and happiness ?"

Eagerly the detective peered forth to obtain a glimpse of the contents of the box, and as he did so—interested as he was—he momentarily forgot the book which lay upon his lap, and which just at this important moment slipped from his knee and fell to the floor with a loud noise.

Archibald MacDonald started suddenly, closing the lid with a sharp snap, and turning around, the detective caught a glimpse of as distorted a visage as had ever met his view.

The fear, the suspicion and the agony of that expression were startling, and the detective, realizing the necessity of prompt action, sank noiselessly back in his chair pretended to be sound asleep.

With quick but stealthy strides the startled man reached the window, and pulling aside the curtains discovered the detective slumbering as peacefully but as uncomfortably as was possible for man to do.

For a moment he stood gazing at the detective, who, schooled in his art, never quivered so much as an eyelid under the searching look that was fastened upon him.

He could hear a profoundly expressed sigh of relief escape the man as he became satisfied of the fact of the unconscious state of the detective, and he hurriedly returned to the table, relocked the box, and restored it to its hiding-place within the secretary.

Having accomplished this he turned to the table, and seizing the decanter poured out a large glass of liquor, and with trembling hand raised it to his lips and drained it at a single swallow.

Further proceedings were interrupted by the entrance of Vernon Barber, who came in shivering with cold and growling at the storm outside.

"I will go with you to Chicago on Thursday," said MacDonald, and then he added in a whisper, "and we will take those things with us."

He then motioned to the position of the detective, and walking to where he was sitting he gently attempted to awaken him.

"Come, Mr. Pinkham, you are taking your nap too early in the day. Come, take something that will open your eyes," he said, very pleasantly, but there was a tremor in his tones which proved that he had not entirely recovered his nerves.

Pinkham roused himself apparently with a great effort, and apologizing to Mr. MacDonald for falling asleep he helped himself to a drink and shortly after left the room.

As he walked to the rear of the house he stood for a few minutes at the open door gazing out at the view presented before him.

Everything without was cold, bleak and cheerless ; the rain came down with a monotonous pour, the dull

6

leaden sky stretched away with no brightening promise of sunshine. The low of the dripping and rain-soaked cattle was borne to his ears, and he could see the disconsolate looking fowls as they shrank into sheltered places, and endeavored to smooth their ruffled plumage.

It appeared as though all the warmth and comfort had faded out of existence.

What caused that sudden start of surprise and that fear-distorted pallid face which he had just seen? Archibald MacDonald was not a coward to be frightened by a sudden noise within his own library. How then to account for the carefulness with which he assured himself of the detective's sleep? Why that self-propounded question:

"Are these things worth a man's honor and happiness?"

As surely as the sun will shine again from those heavy banks of clouds; as truly as the flowers will bloom with added freshness after their invigorating baptism, the cause of Archibald MacDonald's fear will be discovered, and he will not stand alone as the question is asked:

"Are these things worth a man's honor and happiness?"

"Are these things worth a man's honor and happiness?"

CHAPTER XIII.

The Race Track—Speculations and Philosophies—Barber and Mac-Donald do some Betting—Mysterious Conferences—And a Journey Home.

I^T is a warm, sunny day in August and in the city of Chicago, and after my noon-day repast, I was seated in my conveyance on my way to the Driving Park of this " Metropolis of the Prairies."

Having been fully informed of the intention of Vernon Barber and Archibald MacDonald to attend the races that were to take place upon this day, I determined to be there also, in order to ascertain whether I had ever seen either of these men or could identify them, particularly Vernon Barber.

In order that there might be no mistake about the matter, an operative was directed to proceed to the depot in advance of their arrival in the city. He was given an accurate description of the two men, and instructed not to lose sight of them until reaching the Driving Park, where I would be stationed in a convenient position and would thus be enabled to distinguish the two gentlemen whom I was desirous of making the acquaintance of.

A race track is a wonderful place for the study of humanity. All classes, all grades, all characteristics of the human species are here represented. Here is the professional gambler, who will make the tour of the country during the racing season, who will be found at every race track, and whose money will be staked upon every conceivable prospect of profitable chance.

And not only upon chance does he rely to increase his gains. With "the ways that are dark and the tricks which are vain" he is perfectly familar. Horses are not always run to win; a venal driver, a dishonest groom, or a bribed stable-boy, very frequently have a more powerful influence upon the result of the contest than do the noble animals which are driven upon the track. Very often a horse whose condition upon the day before the trial of speed gave full promise of successful competition with those against whom he was to contend, and from that fact had become largely the favorite of the unsuspecting betters, here failed most miserably and incomprehensibly when the actual contest took place.

The jubilant faces of the "professionals" who know who has "been seen" in the meantime, and whose winnings have been safely gathered in, could, perhaps, very readily account for this *unexpected* state of affairs, but the poor dupes who have wagered their scanty earnings upon supposed certainties do not discover until too late, if at all, the process by which their money was taken from them.

Here is the prosperous gentleman, who wagers trifling sums of money or inconsiderable articles of forfeit "just for the fun of the thing," and here a bevy of beautiful ladies, whose rich dresses and sparkling jewels bespeak their position in society, and they, too, catching the infection of the moment, will gayly forfeit gloves or slippers with gentlemanly attendants upon the merits of the horse which has captivated their fancy and rendered them enthusiastic.

There is a hungry-eyed and pinched-faced young man, whose anxiety so plainly expresses a painful story. A wager made yesterday which resulted disadvantageously has made him a thief to-day, and if his favorite horse is a loser, now, disgrace and ignominy will be his portion on the morrow. He laughs and jests with an unquiet air of doubtfulness upon his face, and his hands are nervously pulling at his moustaches as he converses. Ah, miserable young man, down deep in your heart a conflict is raging that in time would wear out the strongest natures and would paralyze the stoutest hearts.

Laugh lightly, your joyous companions will not detect the hollow ring of agony that is manifest in its tones. Laugh loudly, it may serve momentarily to deaden the voice of your reproving conscience, but if this beautiful prancing steed, who is now being so carefully attended by his groom, should be distanced in this contest, go back to your dishonored home, look into the face of your loving, trusting mother, gaze into her eyes and see there the fullness of the sweet confidence and affection that beams upon you, and then, with your hands pressed to your throbbing temples, with your heart weighted as if with lead, go out, and the morning's Gazette will chronicle a mysterious death, a probable suicide. Poor man, it was only a guilty soul seeking release from a bitter remorse, and weakness and crime had culminated in this last dread act.

This is not a new experience, nor is this young man the first who has been tempted who has sinned, and who has died. The Demon of Chance has been abroad in the land long before our day, his gaunt form has stalked through our communities before his existence was known to us, and his victims are as numerous as those of the dreaded Juggernaut.

But hark! the signal is given, and the horses are being led to the stand. Their shining coats and their sleek symmetrical limbs tell unmistakably of the thoroughbred, the flashing of the eyes and the quivering of the nostrils bespeak an instinctive eagerness to struggle for the victory, while the champing at the bit and the nervous stamping of the feet proclaim the impulsive impatience for the trial.

The colored jockeys—for the first race is a running one—with their gay uniforms and brilliant favors, seem as eager as the horses, and as the word is given, away they dash over the smooth ground with a spirit and vim that is fascinating even to the most conservative mind.

Ah, young man, look well now, look intently upon those flying animals. Now hopeful, now anxious, now despairing, again hopeful. Ah, in that brief uncertain period your life is upon trial. Your eyes tell the story, and your beating heart registers the foot-falls of the horses as they speed along. Your fate depends upon the dumb animal that is before you, and what will be the result ?

Meantime I had heard nothing of my operative, and was beginning to grow impatient and somewhat doubtful, when I felt a gentle pressure upon my arm, and then I knew that my gentlemen were within reach.

I had barely time to acknowledge the suggestion given to me, and to turn in the direction in which my operative's eyes pointed me, when I was attracted by the voice of one of the men thus indicated, and who was standing in close proximity to me.

" I will bet one hundred dollars to fifty on the sorrel mare !"

" I'll take it," quickly responded some one in the crowd, and then I turned around and looked full in the face of the first speaker.

He was tall, well-dressed and smooth-faced—a man not calculated to attract a great deal of attention, but there was something in the expression of his face which struck me at once as familiar, and as I furtively watched him, a dawning recollection of the man in other times, and among other scenes, as slowly but vividly, recalled to my mind, and Vernon Barber, at last, was known to me.

Two years prior to this, I had been in the town of St. Catharines upon an operation of considerable importance, which required my personal supervision, and I had located myself at a very agreeable and comfortable hotel in the town, which was kept by a genial fellow, who was at one time a resident of Chicago, and whose name was George May.

The business that I was then engaged upon, had detained me in the town for several days, and George May, the proprietor, and myself, became quite familiar in our intercourse, he, of course, maintaining entire secrecy as to my name and calling. It while here, that a man appeared with a fine drove of horses—evidently from the west—which he was desirous of selling. They were placed in the stable of the hotel, and the prices asked being exceedingly low, and the stock remarkably good, they were soon disposed of.

" I'll guarantee that those horses are not honestly come by," said I, to George May, as a very fine animal had been disposed of, for much less than his real value,

" or else this fellow is very new in the business of a horse-trader."

" I have been thinking the same thing myself," replied Mr. May, with a sly wink, as though he might have known more than he cared to tell.

Nothing, however, occurred, to confirm such a suspicion, until one day, as the last horse was being led away, a stranger stopped suddenly in front of the hotel, and, after critically examining the animal, turned to the people who were standing around, and said :

" Well, I could almost have sworn to that horse. It is a perfect picture of one belonging to a friend of mine in Indiana."

" Whereabouts in Indiana ?" inquired the man, who, in despite of the change in his appearance, I now knew to be Vernon Barber, and who had charge of the horses and their sale.

" Just outside of Oaklands," was the reply, and I could see Barber wince slightly under the innocent gaze of the man who addressed him.

" That can't be the horse, at any rate ; I bought this one in Ohio, and you must be mistaken," he said care-lessly, and then he abruptly left the group, entered the hotel and called for a drink, which he swallowed with evident satisfaction.

A short time after this event occurred, he paid his bill and departed, and as no further inquiries were

6*

made at the time, I paid no attention to the matter, and did not charge my mind with it ; but when, some months later, I heard, incidentally and outside of my business operations, of the stealing of the horses in the neighborhood of Oaklands, I felt satisfied that the horse noticed by the inquisitive stranger in St. Catharines was one of the identical lot, and that Vernon Barber was the thief.

His personal appearance was very much changed since then, and the whiskers which he then wore had disappeared ; but I very seldom, if ever, forget a face, and I was convinced that Vernon Barber, the thief who had robbed Archibald MacDonald and his neighbors of their horses two years ago, and Vernon Barber, the acknowledged friend and guest of Archibald MacDonald to-day, were one and the same person.

Here was food for speculation and of a very annoying character.   While I was rejoiced at being able to know my man and to locate him in a questionable enterprize, his intimacy with Archibald MacDonald perplexed and annoyed me.   To associate him with the previous misdeeds of Vernon Barber, seemed so utterly at variance with his mode of living, and the high character he had always borne in the community in which he resided, that I involuntarily shrank from entertaining the idea.

I resolved, however, to probe the matter, to invest-gate thoroughly and carefully, to strike and fear not, and then, whatever the result, I would be sustained by my own convictions of right, and I would feel that I had performed my full duty.

These thoughts revolved through my mind as I stood gazing at the men before me. All interest in the competing animals was lost. I forgot temporarily all about the nervous young man about whom I had been previously philosophizing.

It mattered little to me, which of the trained runners was the first to reach the goal of victory. I was engaged in another chase which occupied my attention, a chase in which the law's purity had been violated, in which forcible hands had been laid upon the property of others, and in which, I was confident, I could put my hand upon one of the real criminals. Victory of another kind was within my reach, and the excitements and enthusiasm of the scenes around me now failed to interest or amuse.

I realized full well the necessity of the utmost caution and discretion. I appreciated the fact that a false move upon this board would result in defeat. I knew that I must exercise all the care that was possible, and then I felt sure that justice would be done, guilt would be punished, and the law upheld.

As I reached thus far in my reverie, the air was rent with deafening cheers ; from a thousand throats came the

wild cry which told that the race—a four mile dash—
was finished, and that the winner in the struggle was
known.

On came the horses, urged by their drivers with whip
and spur to their utmost efforts, and as the rushing mass
passed under the wire at the judge's station, Vernon
Barber, turning around to the individual with whom he
had made the wager, said in an exulting voice :

"I think, sir, I have won your money; the sorrel is
the winner."

After he had received the money he turned to his
companion, saying :

"Now, Mack, let us go back to the stables. I want
to see if every thing is all right there."

"Very well," replied the other, whom I now knew
to be Archibald MacDonald, and the two men left the
stand and proceeded in the direction named.

Directing my operative to follow these men and report their movements, and having no further interest in
the races that were to follow the one I had only partly
witnessed, I reached my conveyance and was driven back
to my agency.

Vernon Barber, accompanied by his companion, proceeded directly to the stables connected with the driving
park, and soon the first-named individual found himself
surrounded by a number of acquaintances of the frater-
nity of the turf.

Calling aside a man who was prominent in the group, and whose horse was entered for the concluding race of the day's programme, they were soon engaged in earnest conversation. What the nature of it was, however, my operative could not ascertain, as it was carried on in a low tone, and he was unable to approach very near to them without attracting attention.

Whatever the purport of their consultation might have been, it was soon ended, and evidently to the satisfaction of both parties, after which they turned again to the group which they had left, and Vernon Barber, taking the arm of his friend led him away.

"It's all right," said he; "and now let us go and buy some pools."

They reached the booth where the pools were sold, and soon Vernon Barber became an active bidder upon the results of the concluding race of the day. Confidently he made his wagers, and promptly he deposited his money, until from their joint funds the two men had ventured several thousand dollars.

Having satisfied his inclinations in this direction, he again addressed MacDonald, who had been a silent, but decidedly interested party to the proceedings :

" Now, Mack, we will see if we can find anyone who can help us out with these little articles we have to dispose of."

"Barber," said MacDonald in a hesitaitng manner, "I did not bring them with me, I was afraid to."

"Afraid of what, man?" asked Barber, snappishly. "There is nothing to be afraid of," and then he added, with an oath, "We will have to make the best of it and see if we can find any one who will serve us in the future."

After walking about the grounds and through the mass of people, Barber suddenly slapped his companion upon the shoulder, and exclaimed :

"By God, Mack, here is the very man. Come along."

He started through the crowd, half pulling MacDonald after him, and only stopped when within speaking distance of a flashily-dressed individual, who was offering bets in a loud voice to those who stood around him.

This individual was instantly recognized as one of the most successful Bank robbers in existence, and whose skill in disposing of the spoils thus obtained was unequalled.

Barber and this man were evidently old friends, and their greeting was as cordial and hearty as if they were brothers.

Again a whispered conversation took place, in which, MacDonald having been duly introduced, all three took part, and upon its conclusion, the stranger, addressing MacDonald, said, in a voice loud enough for my detective to hear ·

"It will be all satisfactory, and if you will bring them to me, I will see what I can do with them."

The last race, a trotting match, and the one on which Barber and MacDonald had placed their money so eagerly, was now about to start, and the two men turned their attention to the talk.

The horses were driven out, and at the word "Go," were skimming around the circle. Barber evinced no concern, however. Matters were too surely arranged behind the scenes, and the results of the race demonstrated the correctness of his opinion, for the wagers that he had made resulted in his favor, and MacDonald and himself were winners of a large sum of money.

"Not a bad day's work, Mack," said Barber, "and not so risky either as some we know of."

MacDonald shivered a little at this remark, but answered laughingly in the affirmative, and the two men walked toward their conveyance, and drove away from the park very well satisfied with what had been done.

They reached the depot in time, and were soon upon their way home, little dreaming that they had been the subject of strict surveillance, and that detectives were upon their track.

CHAPTER XIV.

AFTER these proceedings had been duly reported to me, I fully made up my mind as to what course to pursue, and I immediately wrote to Mr. Pinkham, giving him my instructions as to his future course of action.

The morning after the races, Barber and MacDonald were early astir, and went out into the fields, where Pinkham was at work with the new machine. Everything had worked admirably, and Mr. MacDonald expressed his gratification at the progress that had been made, and congratulated Pinkham upon the successful operation of the new machine.

The day passed off uneventfully, and in the evening Pinkham, accompanied by Vernon Barber, drove over to Oaklands, for some articles that were needed. Leaving Barber at the store, he called at the post-office, and received my letter. Having read it very carefully, he placed it in his pocket and returned for his companion, and they started upon their return to the residence of Mr. MacDonald.

Pinkham dexterously led the conversation, and soon

gave Barber to understand that he was known to him, and he also mentioned having seen him at St. Catharines, during his horse-selling operations.

Barber evinced considerable surprise at the information thus conveyed, but Pinkham reassured him by informing him that he was once engaged in that business himself, and that he was only pursuing his present business until he could find another safe opportunity of practicing his old profession.

He related to Barber several fictitious incidents of " crookedness," in which he had been concerned, and by the time they had reached their destination, he had completely won the confidence, and even the admiration of the credulous Barber, who expressed a strong desire to become better acquainted with his new-found friend.

" Come in to the library, Pinkham, the night is a little cool, and we will take something to warm us up a little," said he, as they alighted at the door.

As they passed the sitting room, they saw Archibald MacDonald and his wife, seated near the table, and Mrs. MacDonald was engaged in reading a letter to her husband, that day received from Kate, who was to return home in a few days, to prepare for the most important affair of her life.

The wife, as her eyes glanced over the pages of the loving missive, displayed a countenance beaming with the true warmth and love of a mother's heart, and her voice trembled a little as she read to the father of the girl the affectionate messages which the letter contained.

Mr. MacDonald, on the contrary, seemed to be sad and morose. He failed to smile at the little pleasantries which the happy girl indulged in, and he hailed as a relief the entrance of the two men, and quickly accepted their invitation to repair to the library.

Pinkham remained with them but a few minutes, and then, pleading fatigue from the labors of the day, retired to his room.

The next morning, while he was engaged in his agricultural occupation, Vernon Barber came out into the fields, and during the frequent rests that were necessary, indulged in conversation with Pinkham, evidently with the desire of drawing him out and forming an estimate of his character.

Pinkham was not slow to discover this, and his ready wit and varied experiences enabled him to fully satisfy whatever doubts might have been entertained in regard to the qualifications which he possessed for the calling he asserted that he had previously followed.

Barber seemed to be revolving some project in his mind about which he did not appear to be fully determined, and after continuing the conversation for some little time he went away, saying that he would talk with him further that evening.

Pinkham performed his duties faithfully during the day, and after he had changed his clothing and partaken of the evening meal he was requested to join Mr. Barber in the library. Following him into the cosy little room, he soon became convinced that he was on the eve of receiving some information that would be of benefit to him in the investigation he was now engaged in. Nor was he disappointed, for immediately after seating themselves Barber drew his chair toward the detective, and said :

"Mr. Pinkham, I think we can trust you, and at the same time afford you an opportunity of making a little money, if you are disposed to join us."

Pinkham assured the gentleman that he was willing to join him in anything that promised to augment his fortunes, and which possessed the elements of success.

Barber then submitted to him a well-arranged plan for robbing the bank at La Porte. The ground had been fully gone over before and everything was in readiness for the attempt. The watchman at the bank was an old man, who could be readily overpowered and disposed of, and they were provided with all the necessary implements for bursting the safe.

Pinkham listened with intense interest to the proposition thus presented to him, and when Barber had finished he said :

"I will join you, Mr. Barber—the thing looks very

favorable, and I have been engaged before in operations that were a great deal more dangerous; but are two of us enough for this job?"

"Oh, no," replied Barber, "we have a third party all right, he has been over the ground, and knows all about it. He is not here, but he will join us at La Porte, on the night we arrange for the work."

Thus matters were satisfactorily arranged, and my operative found himself engaged in an undertaking which was very foreign to his calling, but which he felt sure would result to the interest of that which had brought him to Oaklands.

Further consultations were held, and finally it was arranged that on the second day following, they should leave Oaklands, and start for the scene of action, where they would be joined by the third party.

On the day appointed, Barber and Pinkham announced their intention of departing by a train which left Oaklands early in the afternoon.

"I think I will run over to Chicago to-day, myself," said Mr. MacDonald. "I have a little business there which requires attention, and I will accompany you part of the way."

"All right, Mack," replied Barber, "we will be glad to have your company."

After dinner the party started off, and were soon

on board the train and upon their journey to the city where their burglarious venture was to be attempted.

Mr. MacDonald accompanied them until they reached the intersection, where he bade them good bye, and left the train. The other two proceeded on their way, and soon reached La Porte in safety, where they went to a hotel and prepared to await the arrival of their confederate.

Of course, I had been fully informed of all these preparations, and my plans had been arranged accordingly. Two operatives met the party upon their arrival, and unobservedly accompanied them to the hotel.

Early in the evening, the expected confederate arrived, and was introduced to Pinkham as Dick Browning.

Pinkham eyed the man suspiciously ; his black hair and full beard were evidently assumed for the occasion, and the dark skin was unnatural in its hue. The man was disguised, but in spite of this fact, Pinkham seemed to be impressed with the idea that the newcomer was known to him. By what means, or under what circumstances, he could not tell, but he instinctively felt that he had been associated with him before.

Ordering a bottle of liquor and some glasses into their room, the three men began to discuss their plans for the night's work.

The satchel which Barber had brought with him contained a full assortment of burglar's tools, and the gags and bucks that might be required, should their work necessitate their use.

Merrily they laughed as they drank, and impatiently awaited the time of the commencement of their nefarious labor.

Laugh on, gentlemen—but there is an old adage, trite and true, that " he laughs best who laughs last."

CHAPTER XV.

Clayton Wolford and Kate MacDonald—A Proposal—Preparations for the Wedding.

WE will now return to the daughter of Archibald MacDonald, who had been so miraculously saved from a dreadful death by the courage and strong arm of Clayton Wolford.

Their acquaintance soon developed into an affection as warm and demonstrative as it was sincere and abiding. To the young man the manifold graces of the young girl appeared as a revelation of the idol of his dreams, and he yielded her the homage of a noble and loving heart—while to Kate the manly courage, the noble bearing, the strong intelligence and honest heart expected separation utterly destroyed her appreciation of all that was entrancing and inspiring in the loveliness of moonlit nature.

She was standing thus when she felt a light touch upon her arm, and Clayton Wolford whispered :

"The evening is too beautiful to remain in-doors, Miss MacDonald ; will you not favor me with a short stroll on the lawn ?"

" With pleasure, Mr. Wolford," replied Kate, as she dashed the little pearly tear-drops from her eyes, and throwing a wrap about her shoulders, she placed her arm within his, and together they walked out into the beauty of the night.

Silently they walked for some time, each occupied with his own thoughts, when Clayton Wolford, disengaging his arm, turned toward Kate, and addressed her.

" Miss MacDonald, I am going away to-morrow. I have already stayed too long, but I could not tear myself away from your side. A strange attraction seemed to keep me near to you. In the time that I have been home, however, I have learned to love you, to love you warmly and devotedly. Tell me, Miss MacDonald— Kate, can you love me in return, and will you be my wife ?"

Kate had looked up into his face as a startled fawn, when he first began speaking ; her glorious eyes sparkled in the moonlight as she heard his declaration, and as he finished, her head sank upon his shoulder, while her frame thrilled with a pleasure she had never known before. Slowly the whispered words came from her beautiful lips, as she murmured earnestly,

" I do love you, Clayton, and I will be your wife— your true, dutiful and loving wife."

Impulsively the young man clasped her in his arms, and imprinted upon her lips a lingering kiss, the first and only one that had been impressed there save by parents and her brother, since she was a little child.

" Heaven bless you, darling, you have made me very happy."

All the sorrow of parting was gone from her heart now, all the gloom which had settled upon her spirits had been lifted by the roseate light of love, and they walked arm in arm toward the house with a strange brilliancy in their eyes, which told of a mutual affection.

The young man's parents were at once informed of what had taken place, and their joy was unmistakably apparent. They had known Kate long and well, and had already learned to love her as a daughter. Clara was delighted, and in her own impetuous way nearly smothered her with kisses.

Clayton immediately informed Mr. MacDonald of his regard for Kate, and made a formal request for her hand, and after a mutual explanation, the consent of her parents had been freely given, and the day of the wed-

7

ding had been fixed for the month of September, in the following year.

It was in the month preceding this that Pinkham paid his visit to Oaklands, and become identified with Vernon Barber in their burglarious attempt at La Porte.

Kate was daily expected home, and it was the letter announcing her speedy return that was being perused on the evening when Vernon Barber and Henry Pinkham returned to the farm-house after their confidential conversation.

Preparations had been in progress for the wedding, and as it was to take place at the residence of Mr. Mac-Donald, his visit to Chicago was accounted for by the necessity of making certain purchases which were required for the approaching important event.

CHAPTER XVI.

The Attempted Burglary—An unexpected Reception—A Desperate Struggle—And a Surprising Revelation.

VERNON BARBER and his companions waited impatiently for the time to arrive when they would start out upon their journey. At length, as the hour drew near, Dick Browning arose, and walking to the window and throwing open the sash, looked out into the dimly lighted streets.

What a night it was ! The rain was falling in a steady pour, the streets were running channels of water, and the gas lights glimmered faintly through the mist and gloom. They could not have selected a more propitious evening for their undertaking. But few pedestrians ventured out, and the streets were almost entirely deserted. Now and then a close covered carriage would rattle past, but save these at occasional intervals the city seemed to be securely housed.

It was also very possible that the guardians of the night, those blue-coated sentries who walk their beats with monotonous regularity, would seek shelter from the elements upon such a night, and the three men congratulated themselves that fate or fortune was certainly in their favor for this time at least.

" Come, Dick," said Barber, " pass the bottle once again, and then we will be moving. I will carry the kit and go out first and you two can follow afterwards."

The glasses were filled and they drank success to their enterprize in a stiff horn of whiskey.

" Now Barber, be off," said Dick Browning, nervously, "and make haste about it. We are losing precious time."

" All right," said Barber, and arising from his seat, he drew on his great coat, and pulling the collar about his ears, he placed the small satchel under his arm, and started off.

In a few minutes afterwards, the two others closely enveloped descended the stairway and left the hotel.

A strong wind was blowing, which drove the rain directly in their faces, but unmindful of this the men trudged on. Barber, who had donned a false beard, several feet in advance, and the other two walking in the rear together.

Noiselessly emerging from a covered way opposite, and at a safe distance, followed an operative of mine, who had been patiently awaiting their appearance. Briskly walked the burglars and stealthily followed the detective, and after a short journey they reached the Bank Building, which stood upon the corner of two intersecting streets, and from the window of which glimmered the faint rays of a low-burning light within.

With stealthy movements the men approached the building, gazing anxiously around ever and anon to assure themselves that they were not observed. They then went to the rear entrance of the bank, and after halting for a few moments, as though to consult upon their plans of action, Barber advanced to the door and prepared to pick the lock.

Steadily the rain fell with a dismal monotony, but, unmindful of this, the two dark forms stood there, while the third crouched before the door.

Uttering an exclamation of satisfaction, Vernon Barber stepped back, and the door swung noiselessly open. Instantly the three men leaped into the passage-way which led directly to the banking room.

As they entered, a shrill noise, which might have been the whistling of the wind, was heard, which was the signal from the outside, and as the burglars, bursting the inner door with their united strength, rushed into the room, they were confronted by four men, revolvers in hand, who stood menacingly before them.

"Surrender, in the name of the law!" thundered the voice of the foremost, as the men cowered before them, surprised and overwhelmed at the unexpected apparition that met their gaze.

Dick Browning was the first to recover himself, and, dropping the satchel which he had taken from Barber, he faced around and started for the door through which they had entered. Too late, however—for the rain-soaked detective who had followed them through the deserted streets, had silently entered, and stood in the door-way, effectually guarding that avenue of escape.

"My God! I am ruined!" exclaimed Browning, and, with the ferocity of a tiger, he desperately rushed upon the officer.

A struggle, fierce and deadly, instantly followed. The reckless man closed upon the operative with a grip of iron, and with herculean strength attempted to hurl him to the floor, but, quick as a flash, one of the others bounded to the rescue, and in a few moments the intrepid burgler was overcome and securely bound, while the others received the same attentions from the remaining officers.

In the encounter which had taken place, the false hair and beard which Dick Browning had worn, became disarranged, and one of my men stepping up to him, forcibly jerked them off.

To the wonderment and dismay, and at the same time the mournful satisfaction of Henry Pinkham, in the swarthy-visaged companion of Barber, now bereft of his hirsute disguise, he beheld the features of Archibald MacDonald, the aristocratic farmer of Oaklands.

With a cry of agony almost heart-rending in its intensity, Archibald MacDonald fell to the floor in a deathly swoon.

Ah, who can tell the dreadful anguish of this man's mind, as he found himself thus a captive in the hands of the law! His beautiful home, his happy wife and loving children—and Kate, the dear daughter of his heart, about to be married—and now ruin, and dishonor, disgrace and ignominy, staring him in the face. It is no wonder that the strong muscles relaxed, the poor sinful heart stood still, and that the overtaxed brain succumbed to the fearful consequences which his guilty actions had entailed upon him.

The mask removed.

The curtain would soon be lifted from the double life he had been leading, and a loving family, faithful friends, and an admiring community would behold in all the deformity of criminal guilt, the man who had been loved, honored, and esteemed.

The two torn pieces of envelope, the one found in the express office at Troyville, and the other at the hotel at the Suspension Bridge, had been of vital importance in this investigation, and it was mainly due to their agency, that the detection of the criminals had been accomplished.

CHAPTER XVII.

The Finding of the Missing Bonds—An Attempted Suicide—A Sad Story of Temptation and Crime—The Prisoners Removed to Troyville.

AFTER laborious efforts, Archibald MacDonald was at length restored to consciousness, and opening his eyes, he gazed vacantly around at the men who stood before him. For a time he seemed scarcely to realize his position, but as the dreadful truth forced itself upon him, he shivered as with cold, and looked up piteously into the faces of the officers, but did not utter a word.

The captured burglars were conducted immediately

to the hotel, where they had taken up their quarters, and from which they had departed but a short time before, with every prospect of success before them.

Back through the storm they walked, and the unceasing rain and the sighing wind, appeared to be in perfect consonance with their feelings. Barber walked with a defiant air, and seemed to be utterly careless of his position or his prospective punishment. MacDonald, on the contrary, appeared to be completely crushed and humiliated by the circumstances which surrounded him—his head sank upon his chest, and he walked with a slow, halting step, almost dragged along by the officers upon either side.

Pinkham followed, accompanied by one of the officers, but as his part in the affair is well known, it may be imagined that he displayed the effrontery of an old offender and conducted himself with nonchalant indifference.

Upon reaching the hotel, the men were taken directly to the room which they had occupied, and an examination of their effects was at once begun.

The satchel which they had carried had been secured, and as has already been stated, contained all the implements that were necessary for the purpose of breaking into the safe, and all the appliances that would be required to successfully secure any individual who might be found upon the premises.

Archibald MacDonald, on preparing to leave the room, in the first instance, had removed his under coat, which was found carelessly thrown upon the back of a chair, and as the officer picked up this garment for the purpose of examining it, he uttered a smothered groan and ineffectually attempted to grasp it in his hands.

This action excited the suspicion of the man, and a careful inspection was made of this article of clothing, when to the intense delight of Pinkham and the officers, they discovered a large package in the inside pocket, which, upon investigation, proved to be the missing bonds that had been stolen from the safe of the Howard Express Company at Troyville.

Upon this discovery, the countenance of Archibald MacDonald underwent a fearful change ; he became livid in the face, his eyes glared with a frenzy that seemed to indicate a tottering reason, while his features twitched spasmodically, as though he was suffering intense agony.

Finally the agonized look passed away, and in its place came an expression of a deep despair and a fixed determination—a look such as gamesters wear when the last dollar has been staked and lost, and ruin is before them—or that is seen upon the face of the criminal as he ascends the scaffold to suffer for his crime.

The discovery of the stolen bonds upon the clothing of Archibald MacDonald settled at once and conclusively

7*

the question as to who were the guilty parties in that
transaction. He had brought these securities with him
to La Porte, intending, after this robbery had been completed, to journey to Chicago and deposit them with the
individual whom they had met at the race track, and
with his assistance the attempt was to be made to alter
and dispose of them.

So quietly had this arrest been conducted that no one
save the persons directly participating in it, had any
knowledge of such an event taking place.

Mr. Bangs was immediately telegraphed for, and,
awaiting his arrival, the men were taken to the prison
and held to await any judicial investigation that was
necessary.

In the morning the capture of the burglars was
widely circulated, and many curious citizens wisely spec-
ulated as to the manner in which the authorities had
been informed of the contemplated burglary so as to be
so well posted and prepared to meet them upon their
entrance.

No information was given of this, however, as it was
designed that no publicity should be made of Pinkham's
connection with the matter. After an interview with
the authorities, however, Mr. Pinkham was quietly
released from confinement without his companions being
informed of the fact.

The next morning as the keeper was passing the

cell to which Archibald MacDonald had been consigned, he noticed that the prisoner was lying upon the floor in a peculiarly cramped and uncomfortable position. Imagining that he had fallen from his low and narrow bed in his sleep, he entered the cell for the purpose of awakening him and of placing him in a more comfortable posture.

Upon turning him over, he was met by the blank, staring expressionless eyes of the prisoner; while a white foam was issuing from the tightly pressed lips, the limbs twitched convulsively, and the man, though utterly unconscious, appeared to be in great physical pain.

Quickly calling for assistance, Mr. MacDonald was placed upon the bed, and a messenger was immediately dispatched for a physician, as it was feared that the man was dying.

Upon the arrival of the physician, he at once pronounced the symptoms to be those arising from arsenical poisoning, and immediately proceeded to apply the remedial agencies used in such cases.

Yes, there was no doubt of the fact, that Archibald MacDonald, succumbing to the fate that had overtaken him, had attempted to end his existence. The weak nature had given way under the fearful weight of dishonor and disgrace which he had brought not only upon himself but upon the loving and confiding members of his family. He saw himself falling from the high place he had occupied in the esteem of his neighbors and friends, and the honorable station he had held in the community in which he resided. He sank beneath the crumbling ruins of his good name and fortune, and vainly sought release from the agonizing struggle by taking his own life.

The exertions of the physician, however, were soon successful, the rigid limbs relaxed, the color came back to the pallid cheeks, the eyes assumed their natural expression, and consciousness returned to the dazed and despairing mind.

With a shudder, as though awakening from a horrid dream, he opened his eyes and gazed wildly about him, but as he perceived his dismal surroundings, and the official garb of the prison authorities, he realized where he was, and raising his hands to his face he wept bitterly.

"Why did you not let me die?" he asked, in a broken, supplicating voice. "My family would at least have been spared the disgrace of a criminal trial and a public condemnation."

His identity had not yet been confided to the prison officials, who still imagined him to be some hardened offender, and they were considerably surprised at this exhibition of feeling and this touching allusion to his family.

With kind words they attempted to assure him, until at last under the influence of the doctor's soothing prescriptions he sank into a heavy slumber.

Before the unfortunate man awoke, Mr. Bangs arrived and went directly to the cell which he then occupied, requesting to be left alone with him until his sleep should be ended, and when at last his slumber had exhausted itself and he again opened his eyes, they rested upon the kindly face of my general superintendent.

Though still very weak, his faculties were entirely restored, and Mr. Bangs by gentle words, soon succeeded in composing his mind, and then led him gradually to speak of himself.

His story is only one of many that might be related, of those who have chosen the path of crime and have suffered the penalties of detection.

"I was born," said he, in a voice that was feeble at first, but which grew stronger as he proceeded, "in Scotland. My father was an industrious and well-to-do farmer, and I received the benefit of a good education, and my mother, who is now dead, thank heaven, loved me devotedly. As I grew up into manhood I was seized with an uncontrollable desire to come to America. My studies became irksome and distasteful, and my labor on the farm at home seemed very hard and unremunerative, and at last, my father, after frequent entreaties, yielded his objections, and consented that I should seek my fortune in the States.

"Provided with a liberal outfit and with a sum of

money equal to my present wants, I bade farewell to the old home, and with my mother's kiss upon my lips and her tears upon my cheek, I sailed away from the land of my birth, crushing the tears back from my own eyes as ambitious dreams of future wealth flitted before me.

"After an uneventful voyage I landed at Philadelphia, and at the hotel where I stopped in that city, I made the acquaintance of a prosperous and liberal-hearted farmer, whose land lay in Chester Valley in the State of Pennsylvania. After several conversations with him it was arranged that I should enter his service, and as I was fully conversant with the science of farming, and worked diligently, I soon obtained his favor, and my life under his roof and in his service passed pleasantly and happily away.

"It was here that I met the lady whom I afterwards married," and here his voice grew husky with emotion, "and after my marriage, I bought a little farm of my own, where we lived happily together. Two children were born to us, a boy and a girl, and as they grew in years, I began to grow dissatisfied with my humble position and the slow accumulation of money. I longed to be rich, to be enabled to send my children to institutions where they would be educated to adorn the high place in society which I designed for them. I wanted to give additional comforts and luxuries to my loving and devoted wife, and under such reflections, I soon grew discontented with my lot, and longed for a change.

"It was while my mind was in this condition, that I met Vernon Barber. He was a young man apparently with plenty of money, and with no serious cares. He came into our neighborhood during one summer, and remained through the warm weather of July and August. He was a gay, careless fellow, and we soon became intimate friends. To him I communicated my dissatisfaction with my situation, and my desires for the increase of my wealth. He told me I was foolish to work so hard when I could make money much easier, and finally, in a moment of weakness, I listened to his tempting arguments, and joined with him in the stealing of some horses from the farmers in the adjoining county. He undertook the entire charge of disposing of them, and in a few days he returned, and handed me three hundred dollars as my share of the proceeds.

"After that time, however, I began to withdraw myself from my neighbors, a guilty conscience made me a coward, and I imagined that I was suspected of the act I had committed. My life, in consequence, became very aggravating and unpleasant. I then heard of the farm in Indiana, which I afterwards purchased, and remove to with my family.

"Vernon Barber kept up his intimacy with me, and visited me several times. During his visits he pictured to my mind in glowing colors, the ease and safety with which other efforts of a dishonest nature could be accomplished, and having participated with him once before, I was easily induced to join with him again.

" My children were now of an age when they required higher educational advantages than I could have afforded them by legitimate means, and being desirous for their advancement, I was soon identified with many adventures which resulted profitably, and without danger.

" In company with two others we robbed my neighbors of several valuable horses, and in order that no suspicion might attach to me, it was arranged that my barn should also be entered and one of my best horses taken.

" This was successfully accomplished, and the horses were driven to the lake shore, where they were conveyed by boat to Canada, and successfully disposed of.

" So thoroughly schooled had I become in the art of deception, that I actually led the pursuit of the thieves and the attempt to recapture out property.

" Time passed on, and at length he came to me and proposed the robbery of the Express Company's safe at Troyville. His description of the place, the ease with which the matter might be accomplished, and the surety of gaining a large sum by the operation, were too tempting, and I consented to join with him in that undertaking. Of the result of that venture you are already aware, and how disastrous it has been to me, you also know full well.

" Then came this last attempt, and, with its failure, I am brought face to face with disgrace and dishonor, and my family, innocent and unsuspecting as they are, will be compelled to suffer for my misdeeds."

As he finished his recital, the strong man bowed his head in his hands and sobbed loudly. He had told his story brokenly and with faltering voice, but he seemed to feel as though its relation would bring relief. Much more was related, but the important facts as they are connected with the operation in hand, only have been preserved.

It was truly a pitiable spectacle, and Mr. Bangs was deeply moved as he listened.

Sympathy, however, could avail nothing in the present instance, the law must take its course, and, being provided with the necessary papers for their apprehension upon the Howard Express robbery, the next day they were taken to Troyville, and, upon a preliminary hearing, were held over to await their trial.

CHAPTER XVIII.

The News at Oaklands—A Letter and its Contents—A Daughter's
Sacrifice and a Mother's Grief.

THE news of the arrest of Archibald MacDonald
and Vernon Barber was not slow in reaching
the quiet precincts of Oaklands. The daily journals
contained the important announcement, and the little
village was soon in a state of wild excitement. At first
a prevailing sentiment of surprise and regret was manifested, but gradually the jealous minded and the envious,
those who had noted the success of Archibald MacDonald with selfish distrust, began to give voice to their
long pent-up animosities.

With wise looks and shrugging shoulders they stated
that they had always thought there was something wrong
about this man, they had always felt that he was not
what he ought to have been, and now that the revelation
had come, startling as it was, it was only the realization
of what they had long expected and fully believed would
be the eventual result.

Through all this expressed opposition to Archibald
MacDonald, however, there was a prevalent and deep-
seated feeling of sorrow and sympathy for his disgraced
and innocent family.

The quiet, gentle wife was known and admired by every one, and Kate's radiant beauty and winsome ways had made her many friends in the community in which her parents resided. Many were the words of regret that were uttered for these members of the dishonored man's family.

"Poor lady," said one, "this will be a sad blow to her."

"Yes," replied another, "and Kate, too. She came home the other day looking so bright and happy. I am afraid this will be dreadful news for her."

"Poor girl," added a third, "and she was going to be married soon, I hear—a sorrowful wedding this will be."

While they were thus talking, a man from MacDonald's farm drove up to the store, and instantly a dead silence fell upon the assembled group.

The man looked curiously around at the unwonted crowd and seemed at a loss to account for the unusual gathering. No one vouchsafed any information, however, but his salutations were received with a restraint and formality which told him that something more than common had occurred.

He said nothing nor did he ask any questions, but receiving his letters, he left the store and drove toward home.

At the farm-house, matters were in their usual comfortable condition. Mrs. MacDonald sat in her cosy rocking-chair, busily engaged in sewing upon some white article of apparel, evidently intended for the wonderful event that was to take place during the fol-following month. Kate was seated at the piano, and her rich, full voice floated out upon the summer air, with a volume of harmony that would have ravished the ears of an appreciative listener. She was joyous and happy, and the melody she sang, was one of those bright little trifles, that seemed to have been written for the relief of an exuberant joy.

The sound of approaching horses, and the rattle of wheels, informed them of the return of the man with the eagerly expected letters, and Kate, hastily arising from her musical occupation, ran out on the porch to receive the loving messages she was fondly expecting from the absent lover.

The man handed her the packet, saying as he did so :

" There must be something the matter over at the village."

" Why do you think so ? " inquired the unsuspecting girl.

" Because there was a great crowd gathered about the store, and they seemed to be talking about something very important. When I came up, though, they stopped, and I didn't ask any questions."

" We will know all about it in good time," said Kate,

" village news is never slow in traveling," and then she ran lightly into the house.

"Here, mother, is a letter to you from pa, and you can read yours, while I am reading mine," said she, as she handed the letter to her mother.

Kate went to one of the windows, and seating herself in a low chair, hastily removed the enclosure of the letter which she had received, and eagerly devoured its contents.

Scarcely had she commenced her pleasing task, when she was startled by a cry of pain, and turning around, she saw that her mother had fallen from her chair, still holding fast to the letter which she had been reading.

Filled with alarm, the girl hastened to her side, and raising her from the floor, carried her to a lounge and laid her down. Scarce knowing what she did, she flew to the rear of the house and alarming the servants, soon brought them to her aid.

Restoratives were at once applied, and soon returning consciousness came to the fainting woman, when winding her arms around the girl who knelt by her side, she gave vent to her feelings in a copious flood of tears.

Kate, in a state of bewilderment, instinctively took the letter from the hand of her mother, and essayed to read the information which it contained, but the mother, reaching out her trembling hand as if to prevent such action, said :

"No, Kate, not yet. Do not read that letter for a little while, you will know all about it soon enough."

The tone in which she spoke was strained and unnatural, and a strange chill about the heart affected Kate, as she listened. She felt that she was upon the eve of some fearful calamity, but what it was, she could not tell.

After a while the mother roused herself, and directing the servants to leave the room, she took Kate's hands in hers, and, with a firmness that was heroic, she told her the sad news which the letter contained.

Archibald MacDonald had written to his wife the full particulars of his arrest, and of the discovery of his complicity with other crimes. With many affectionate expressions, he had laid bare the whole story of his life, and, alone with her daughter, the despairing and agonized mother related the sorrowful history, concealing as much as was possible of the sickening details, and only acquainting her with the actual facts.

Kate listened in silence, but the light fled from her eyes, and the color from her cheeks, as the recital progressed. In this revelation she saw the bright dream of her life dissipated, the sweet joy of her prospective married life was crushed, and she realized that she must give up the lover to whom she had plighted her troth, and who loved her so devotedly.

The future seemed dark and dismal and forbidding, but she faced it heroically, and she resolved to sacrifice herself rather than bring dishonor upon the fair fame and name of Clayton Wolford.

When the mother had finished, she arose, walked mechanically toward the little writing desk, and, seating herself before it she hurriedly wrote :

"Dear Clayton :

"Our marriage can never take place. Do not ask for a reason ; you will learn too soon that all must be at an end between us.

"Still lovingly yours,

"KATE."

Without pausing to read again the words she had written, she enclosed the note in an envelope, and, hastily directing it, she summoned a servant and dispatched him to the post-office.

Then, turning toward her mother, she clasped her in her arms, and with a face full of trust and patient resignation, she said :

"Mother, we will bear this burden together. You are my father's wife and I am his daughter. We will face this dreadful trial like true women, never forgetting what he has been to us, and what we should be to him."

She had made the sacrifice, and come what would, she was resolved to be true to her woman's nature, and to her love for her father. Deeply feeling the disgrace which he had brought upon himself and them, she never faltered in her duty to her parent, but resolved to visit him at once, and to comfort and sustain him in the terrible hour of his trial.

———◆———

CHAPTER XIX.

The Trial and Conviction—An Attempted Escape—The Death of Archibald MacDonald.

THE trial of Archibald MacDonald and Vernon Barber was held in due course of time, and a large concourse of people assembled to hear the interesting details—some actuated by a strong motive of sympathy toward the unfortunate man and his family, but many, it is feared, came simply to gratify a morbid curiosity and an appetite for the sensational.

As the bowed and stricken man entered the court room, accompanied by his devoted wife and by Frank and Kate, whose faces bore the traces of intense mental anguish, a murmur of pity and sympathy involuntarily burst from the vast assembly.

Could this pallid, emaciated and broken man be the proud and happy farmer of whom they had heard so much, and who had been honored and esteemed by his associates in the days gone by ? Yes, Archibald Mac-Donald was much changed indeed. The silent struggles of the breaking heart and broken spirit, the long confinement, and the accusing voice of conscience that came to him as he thought of the dear ones of his home and heart, to whom he had brought this deep dishonor, has had a marked effect upon the once robust frame of the criminal. He tottered into the court-room, his head bowed down and his limbs trembling under him. Verily, he was paying a dreadful penalty for the few fleeting years of pleasure which he had gained by his dishonest practices.

It is unnecessary to linger over the details of the formal trial. Witnesses were produced who distinctly remembered the two men and identified them as the same which had lodged at the hotel on the night of the robbery ; the two torn pieces of envelope which had led us to the residence of Archibald MacDonald were submitted, and the stolen bonds were offered as convincing evidence that the men now upon their trial were guilty of the offenses of which they were charged.

The evidence was overwhelming, and after a very few moments of deliberation the jury rendered a verdict of guilty, and they were each sentenced to long terms of imprisonment.

Vernon Barber, upon the trial and during his con-

8

finement, had conducted himself with a degree of carelessness and indifference that fully accorded with his reckless nature. He jested incessantly at his companion in crime, and seemed to regard a conscience as worthy only the possession of cowards and weaklings.

By this time, too, he had surmised the true occupation of Henry Pinkham, and his rage at having been so successfully led into the net spread by the detective, was unbounded. He vowed eternal vengeance against Pinkham and Mr. Bangs, but as we are continually being made the subject of such threats on the part of law breakers, they paid no attention to the idle words of the imprisoned malefactor.

On the morning succeeding the trial, Vernon Barber complained of severe pains in his stomach, and requested that he should be furnished with some whiskey. This was handed to him in a cup, and then turning his back upon the keeper, he dropped into the liquor a quantity of lime which he had scraped from the walls of his cell, and which he had mixed with the pepper that had been furnished him with his meals.

After doing this he turned again and advancing toward the unsuspecting official he held the cup before him, saying :

"What kind of stuff is that to give to a sick man ? there is a roach or something else in this cup."

The keeper stooped over to examine the contents of

the vessel, when quick as a flash Vernon Barber threw the liquor full in his face. The lime and pepper, together with the whiskey, entering the eyes of the man completely blinded him and rendered him almost crazy with the pain.

Barber paid no attention to his suffering, however, but putting on his hat, he stood over the prostrate and writhing form of the keeper, and walking to a window that overlooked the enclosing yard of this primitive and insecure place of confinement, he jumped out and strode rapidly away.

The alarm was soon given, and pursuit was at once commenced.

Mr. Bangs was still in the town, and to him the sheriff at once applied for assistance. Accurate descriptions of the man, were at once printed, and men were soon mounted to scour the country in all directions, the telegraph was put into active operation, and before nightfall, the crestfallen thief found himself again a prisoner, and under a guard that would prevent any further attempt to regain his liberty.

The two men were afterwards removed to the State institution, where they were to serve the terms of their imprisonment, and the property of Archibald MacDonald was attached for the payment of the remainder of the money and valuables stolen from the Howard Express Company. This action, however, was found to be unnecessary, as Mrs. MacDonald voluntarily yielded up the property of her husband to satisfy the claims of those whom he had wronged.

Archibald MacDonald did not live to complete his term of imprisonment. He gradually grew more feeble, and at last consumption settled upon him, and within a year of his trial, surrounded by his faithful and grief stricken family, he passed away from earth, a weak victim to avarice and suffering, under the chastening hand of the law.

Of Vernon Barber, I have heard nothing since, whether he be alive or dead I do not know; with the completion of this trial, he passed out of my notice, and he never crossed my path again. I trust, however, that he has reformed from the error of his ways, and though the dark episode of his younger days, in which Miriam Brandon sacrificed life and honor through her love for him, will always be recalled to him, I indulge in the hope, that if still alive, he is endeavoring to lead an honest existence.

CHAPTER XX.

Conclusion.

B UT little now remains to be told, and that little relates to the family of Archibald MacDonald.

After the conclusion of the trial, the sorrowing family returned to the home now made desolate by the sins of the husband and father. But it was home no longer —all the tender memories that had clustered around the happy homestead had been dissipated, and all the brightness and luxury which had been a source of pleasure and enjoyment, were now darkened by the awful shadow of a prison.

And so the estate was sold, the proceeds devoted, as far as could be ascertained, to reimbursing those who had been despoiled ; after which the poor, broken-hearted mother and her children left Oaklands, never to return.

They removed to a distant city, where they remained until the death of Archibald MacDonald, and then, Frank MacDonald, who had now completed his studies, bidding adieu to his mother and sister, departed for the far west, where his antecedents were unknown, and where he could practice the profession for which he was so eminently fitted. Fortune favored him, and to-day he is securely established in a lucrative practice, surrounded by a happy wife (she who once was Clara Wolford) and children, whose loving companionship and gentle ministrations have made him almost forget the dark hours through which he had once passed.

Kate, who had so nobly resolved to relinquish her lover, remained with her mother, and together they fought the battle of life. Clayton Wolford made several attempts to visit her but was invariably refused an interview—the crushed and bleeding heart of the heroic girl could not bear the trying ordeal which she knew would follow, and therefore, with polite firmness, she declined to see the man to whom her love had been given so freely and who was now only the more dear to her because of the gulf between them.

Clayton Wolford, after his last repulse, returned sorrowfully home, devoted himself assiduously to his profession, and attempted to seek forgetfulness by engrossing himself with the growing cares and perplexities of a large and remunerative practice.

Upon hearing of the decease of Kate's father, he resolved to make one more effort to see her ; to convince her that all through her sad trials, his heart had remained true and his love firm.

By diligent inquiries, he ascertained where they resided, and reaching the house, he knocked at the door of their humble abode, when, to his surprise and inexpressible joy, it was opened by Kate herself.

Avoidance of an interview was now quite impossible, and Clayton Wolford at once entered the house.

But I will not linger over the scene that ensued. Clayton's earnest pleadings, and Kate's firm refusal. How he sasured her that it was herself who was dear to him, and that though all the world should frown, he was willing, anxious and determined, to make her his wife.

It is enough to know, that yielding at length to the noble, earnest man, who so tightly held her heart in his keeping, her consent was gained, and they were married. The parents of Clayton received his wife with all the friendship and love that had marked their early intercourse with her—and to-day no happier home is to be found under the blue skies of heaven, than that of the wealthy and honorable lawyer, Clayton Wolford, whose destinies are presided over by his beautiful wife, and the mother of his children, Kate MacDonald—and where, in comfort and peacefulness, the last days of Archibald MacDonald's widow passed contentedly away.